NPS
New Production System
JIT Crossing Industry Boundaries

NPS
New Production System
JIT Crossing Industry Boundaries

Isao Shinohara

Foreword by Norman Bodek, President

Productivity, Inc.

Productivity Press

CAMBRIDGE, MASSACHUSETTS

NORWALK, CONNECTICUT

Productivity Press   Productivity, Inc.
P.O. Box 3007   or   101 Merritt 7 Corporate Park
Cambridge, MA 02140   Norwalk, CT 06851
(617) 497-5146   (203) 846-3777

Library of Congress Catalog Card Number: 87-43310
ISBN: 0-915299-21-6

Book and cover design by Joyce C. Weston
Typeset by Rudra Press, Cambridge, Massachusetts
Printed and bound by Arcata/Halliday
Printed in the United States of America

Library of Congress Cataloging-in-Publication Data

Shinohara, Isao, 1942-
  New production system.

  Translation of: NPS no kiseki.
  1. Production management — Japan. I. Title.
TS155.S48413   1988   658.5   87-43310
ISBN 0-915299-21-6

88 89 90 10 9 8 7 6 5 4 3 2 1

Contents

Table of Illustrations

Publisher's Foreword

W<small>HAT</small> do a garment factory and a prefabricated home component plant have in common? Production-floor workers at Misawa Homes' plant in Matsumoto, Japan, found out one day when their plant was toured by a group of female workers from the World company, a fashion clothing manufacturer located next door. The Misawa Homes workers — men with 20 years of manufacturing experience — were dumbfounded when these much younger workers from a very different type of factory pointed out myriad problems they observed offhand in Misawa's production lines. They were "just garment workers" — what did they know about making prefab houses?

What the seamstresses from World knew about was the New Production System (NPS), a method of production improvement that is not limited to any industry type. Its principles are so universal, in fact, that the consortium which teaches and practices NPS takes only one company per industry for membership.

The New Production System Research Association is the most successful just-in-time consulting group in Japan today. Its methods incorporate the ideas of Taiichi Ohno, the "father" of the famous Toyota production system. Ohno had long believed that the systems he painstakingly developed during his long tenure at Toyota could be used to help any manufacturing industry cut its wastes and improve productivity. Soon after leaving Toyota in 1978, Ohno began the NPS group, joining forces with Kikuo Suzumura, who under Ohno's tutelage had led the just-in-time conversion team at Toyota, and Mikiya Kinoshita, the former president of Ushio, to put his ideas to the test.

Ohno's hunch was clearly correct, as shown by the fascinating examples in this book. Using sometimes drastic means, Suzumura and other members of the Implementation Committee he trained have visited many types of factories, applying basic principles to completely change entire production systems. To date, over 34 companies — many of which had been facing bankruptcy — have applied the NPS method to become successful competitors in their fields. Many more would like to join them.

NPS: Crossing Industry Boundaries is the hottest-selling management book in Japan today. Not long ago, I asked Kikuo Suzumura to tell me the secrets of his success. He said, "The NPS doesn't give interviews. If you want to know more, buy the stock of any NPS company, because they're all going to go up."

Some readers may sense that the idea of NPS is a lot of hype — the bombastics of its instructors, the desperate company presidents going down on their knees to show their commitment to following the system. Yet there is substance beneath this external wrapper — a technique that has increased the profitability of an impressively diverse array of companies, a method as applicable to an electronic parts maker as to a fast-food restaurant.

The NPS concept has profound implications for American business in the 1990s. We have seen the competition, and it is growing smarter. We can no longer afford to say, "Those improvement methods may work fine in a car plant, but they have nothing to do with *my* type of operation." NPS demonstrates that differences in the product or the operation are no excuse for the waste that goes on in most manufacturing plants — beginning with the waste of inventory, something many American companies take for granted. This book should go a long way in reshaping that attitude, and it is with hope and good wishes that I present it to you.

I would like to acknowledge the efforts of a number of people in preparing the English version of this book. Toyo Keizai Shinposha, the original publisher, kindly permitted us to translate the book and provided helpful information during the editorial process. Adex provided the original translation from the Japanese. I would like to thank Karen Jones and Julie Mines, who edited the text and figures; Reiko Kano, who reinterpreted a number of difficult passages; Esmé McTighe, who coordinated book production; Joyce Weston, who designed the book and cover; Marie Kascus, who compiled the index; and the production staff of Rudra Press — Caroline Kutil, Michele Seery, and Susan Cobb.

Norman Bodek

Editor's Note

*T*HE U.S. dollar figures that follow financial information given in Japanese yen are approximations intended to give the Western reader a relative sense of the amounts discussed; they are not represented as firm equivalents of the yen amounts. As the original Japanese publication is copyright 1985, the rate in effect on January 2, 1985 was used for most of the yen amounts. If the yen figure was specifically linked to a different year, the rate for the first business day of that year was used.

Preface

*P*EOPLE are creatures with ties to the past, adopting new things carefully — usually with hesitation and reluctance. They may even reject new things altogether. This is especially true when it comes to changing practices and habits that have been acquired over the years by experience. When people are told that such practices and habits are mistaken, they usually react with anger and distress. It usually takes time to shed the old and accept the new.

Some middle-aged and elderly people — the World War II generation — refer to the younger generation as "strangers," "aliens from another planet," or "the UFO generation." The older generation say that they cannot understand what the young are thinking, what their lifestyle is about, or the language that they use.

The truth of the matter, I think, is not that they cannot understand the young but that they refuse to understand them or refuse to admit that they do understand them. The older generation may be afraid of accepting the world of the young because doing so may reveal to them how old-fashioned and obsolete their world has become.

The corporate environment has changed greatly. The period of high economic growth is now history. It has been replaced by a period of low, stable growth. Consumers — once driven to buy anything new by memories of shortages — are now, in the present abundance, content to buy only what is necessary —

and only in the amount necessary — and only when it is necessary. There is no need to rush out and buy things. They know that they can walk down to the nearest 24-hour convenience store at any time of the day and buy most of their daily essentials. There is no need to waste space in their small homes by storing things. One reason that it is now harder to sell things may be that things are always available.

However, believing the notion that "mass production reduces cost and reduced cost increases market competitiveness," manufacturers continue to increase production, not paying much attention to changes in market conditions and needs. This results in yet more goods flooding the market. Because not all goods can be sold, their price goes down. When the price plunges, manufacturers try to increase production further in order to reduce production costs. A vicious cycle is set in motion. This sequence of events may help to explain what is occurring today.

The New Production System (NPS) teaches us to produce only as many goods as have actually been sold. The NPS does not tolerate speculative production, that is, producing in quantities that are theoretically expected to be sold. Producing only as many goods as have been sold, however, is difficult. Keeping track of how many of which products have been sold or consumed in the market is not easy. Moreover, those at the production end usually resist the policy of producing only as many goods as have been sold. They will usually protest vehemently, saying that producing in small lots only consumes more labor and time, reduces efficiency, and raises costs.

I am sure this is true of any company, but an attempt to start something new at a company is met with strong opposition. Some managers and experienced workers say that "those without experience should keep quiet." Others fear that the success of a new method or idea will embarrass them or reduce their value.

It must be accepted, however, that times are changing. We must give serious thought to what can be done for a better future instead of trying to cling to the past. For this, it may be necessary to look at one's self with a critical eye instead of worrying about being criticized by others.

The philosophy of NPS is to reevaluate business-management methods from the very root. The object of NPS is to achieve *super-rationalization* and *super-efficient management* by a reversal of the ordinary thinking processes.

The presidents of the companies who belong to the NPS Research Association (NPS Kenkyu Kai) consider themselves fortunate to have joined NPS.

I express my sincerest appreciation to Director Mikiya Kinoshita of the NPS Research Association, Chairman Kikuo Suzumura of the association's Implementation Committee, and to all others for their assistance in writing this book. I also apologize for the fact that some of the people mentioned in this book are occasionally referred to without their proper titles.

Isao Shinohara

NPS
New Production System
JIT Crossing Industry Boundaries

PART ONE

A Corporate Group Emerges from Secrecy

CHAPTER ONE

Challenging Matsushita and Toyota

A LARGE, very powerful corporate group is now emerging in Japan. Because the group has remained obscure, it has been undetected, remaining underground like a secret organization. Most people have never heard its name. However, the group is steadily strengthening ties among its member companies.

To venture a bold guess, I confidently predict that this new corporate group will overtake and surpass such leading Japanese conglomerates as the Hitachi group, the Matsushita group, and the Toyota group before the year 2000. It may happen sooner. Many who hear this prediction will say this is impossible, but an incredible miracle is taking place among the companies in this emerging competitor.

Hitachi, Japan's largest electrical manufacturer, had sales of ¥3.0003 trillion ($12 billion) and ordinary profit of ¥158 billion ($628 million) in fiscal 1985. The Hitachi group is a huge conglomerate whose consolidated sales were ¥5.01 trillion ($20 billion) with an expected ordinary profit of ¥371 billion ($1.5 billion).

In 1985 the Matsushita group, with Matsushita Electric Industrial at the core, comprised a total of 82 companies and included such blue-chip firms as Matsushita Communication Industrial, Kyushu Matsushita, Matsushita-Kotobuki Electronics Industries, and Victor Company of Japan. The annual sales of Matsushita Electric Industrial alone were ¥3.4241 trillion ($13.6 billion) in fiscal 1985. The consolidated figures for the Matsushita group showed an annual sales of ¥5.52 trillion ($22 billion) for fiscal 1985 and an ordinary profit of ¥689 billion ($2.7 billion).

In the auto industry, Toyota, which leads second-place Nissan by a wide margin in earnings, had sales of ¥6.3 trillion ($31 billion) and an ordinary profit of ¥500 billion ($2.5 billion) for the period ending in June 1986. These figures for Toyota are tops among all Japanese corporations. Toyota's high profitability and strong financial condition are a matter of public knowledge. Consolidated sales of the Toyota group were ¥7 trillion ($35 billion) and its consolidated ordinary profit just shy of ¥700 billion ($3.5 billion).

It challenges common sense to believe that some new corporate group will be able to overtake and surpass such established, giant conglomerates as Matsushita, Hitachi, and Toyota in little over ten years. It is natural to dismiss such an idea as unrealistic — and in Japanese society, it is especially difficult to dislodge an established system. Established forces apply tremendous pressure on any newcomer trying to grow large. This is even more true when one's competition includes the dominant industrial conglomerates like Hitachi, Matsushita, and Toyota. It is perfectly reasonable to dismiss any notion that some obscure new group will be able to outdo such existing industrial giants.

It is nevertheless true that this corporate grouping is seriously working to become No. 1 in Japan in terms of sales and, more importantly, in terms of profitability. The group has set as its ultimate objective the incredible goal of an ordinary profit equal to 25 percent of sales. Furthermore, it says that its competition is not Hitachi or Matsushita but Toyota. So, this obscure corporate group intends to challenge and surpass Toyota, the leader of the world's auto industry. It must be remembered that the group does have strength and is not simply making idle threats.

This obscure group, this secret organization, is none other than the New Production System (NPS) Research Association, which is also referred to by its Japanese equivalent, Shin Seisan Hoshiki. The association inherits its philosophy from Taiichi Ohno, the former vice-president of Toyota who developed the Toyota production system and is credited with single-handedly leading Toyota to its present eminence as a serious challenger of Ford and General Motors (GM). The purpose of the NPS Research Association is to further develop Ohno's philosophy and to promote "super-rationalized management."

NPS's motivation to surpass Toyota and become a global corporate group will be discussed later. However, it is a fact that the NPS Research Association has Toyota in mind and that Toyota, while remaining outwardly calm and seemingly indifferent, has a keen interest in its activities.

Self-Multiplication Has Started

The NPS Research Association in 1985 comprised 34 member companies. In the beginning, Kibun, famous for its boiled-fish paste products, was the only member company that was relatively well known. The other members were five small businesses. However, membership grew to its current size in only a few years. The aggregate sales of the member companies are now ¥1.5 trillion ($6 billion). The largest company is Nippon Light Metal with annual sales of ¥250 billion ($994 million), followed by Kibun with ¥190 billion ($755 million), Yokogawa Hokushin Electric with ¥180 billion ($715 million), and Misawa Homes and World each with ¥140 billion ($556

MIP Co., Ltd. (Capital: ¥127 million); President: Mikiya Kinoshita; Address: Ichikawa Building, 5-13-3 Ginza, Chuo-ku, Tokyo; Telephone: 03 (545) 1851

Date of Membership	Company	Representative	Capital (millions of yen)	Sales (millions of yen)	Employees	Main Line of Business
January 1981	Oiresu	Seiichiro Azuma	450	20,200	665	Oil-less bearings
January 1981	Kibun	Masahito Hoashi	692	192,000	4,200	Fish-paste products
January 1981	Ogura Hoseki Seiki	Koozaburo Ogura	50	3,000	310	Industrial jewels, acoustic products
January 1981	Ikuyo	Masayoshi Sakai	100	11,000	350	Rubber, synthetic resin products
January 1981	Yoga Seiko	Osamu Hisayama	1,000	1,200	105	Telecommunication equipment
March 1981	Shinshin Shokuryo	Maki Kagoshima	160	19,000	350	Food products
April 1981	• Yokogawa Hokushin Electric	Shozo Yokogawa	11,357	139,000	5,500	Industrial instruments
December 1981	• Skylark	Tasuku Chino	1,425	72,805	2,211	Family restaurants
April 1982	Ishikawa Gasket	Itsuo Ishikawa	200	5,550	270	Automotive parts
April 1982	Nippon Atsudenki	Fuminori Sato	210	10,000	450	Electrical acoustic products, wireless equipment
September 1982	Hokusei Aluminum	Takeo Sato	1,000	26,000	625	Light metal casting and rolling
December 1982	• Ihara Koatsu Tsugite	Tsutomu Ihara	500	9,000	383	Couplings, valves
December 1982	• Nipponcoinco	Masaharu Okada	3,027	12,500	320	Coin-operated mechanisms
January 1983	Asia Securities Printing	Morio Ueno	4,800	1,600	120	Financial printing
January 1983	Showa Denki Kogyo	Michio Ura	160	16,000	560	Design and building of electrical installations
January 1983	• Kawasaki Electric	Noboru Kawasaki	640	10,100	416	Electrical equipment (mainly switchboards)
January 1983	Hokusei Nikkei Katei Yohin	Kenzo Kasama	400	10,000	372	Aluminum household goods

Date of Membership	Company	Representative	Capital (millions of yen)	Sales (millions of yen)	Employees	Main Line of Business
June 1983	• Okamoto Machine Tool Works	Taizo Hosoda	3,049	17,200	520	Machine tools, grinding machines
October 1983	• Nozawa	Taichiro Nozawa	1,000	16,200	618	Corrugated slates, boards
November 1983	World	Hirotoshi Hatasaki	920	120,700	2,163	Women's, men's, and children's apparel
January 1984	• Nippon Light Metal	Hosuke Asano	25,300	279,800	4,874	Aluminum smelting, light pressed goods
May 1984	Showa Maruto	Isao Sato	50	12,500	66	Paper tubes for magnetic tapes
September 1984	• Misawa Homes	Chiyoji Misawa	4,397	126,200	1,158	Prefabricated homes
October 1984	• Bando Chemical Industries	Shigeo Ichiki	3,700	48,000	2,015	Belts and industrial goods
February 1985	Asahi Tokushu Gohan	Torakazu Kaibori	550	12,600	473	Plywood
February 1985	• Shizuki Denki Seisakusho	Kiyokazu Ootsu	1,817	12,100	220	Film capacitors
May 1985	• Hokuetsu Kogyo	Masao Ishida	1,001	23,000	660	Air compressors
May 1985	Nippon Filing	Enpei Tajima	35	11,100	520	Steel cabinets and other storage systems
February 1986	• Noritsu	Toshiro Ohta	5,460	60,500	1,585	Gas furnaces, hot water equipment
February 1986	Kurinappu	Noboru Inoue	1,635	51,000	1,929	Bathroom cabinets, kitchen cabinets
February 1986	Shintokogio	Yuzuru Nakai	2,618	28,900	993	Foundry plant
February 1986	Supankurito Seizo	Yoshihiro Murayama	230	3,000	140	Secondary concrete products
May 1986	• Uni Charm	Keiichiro Takahara	2,312	82,000	476	Paper diapers, sanitary products
May 1986	Shin Nikkei	Shohei Kawakami	3,000	143,500	2,157	Aluminum sash

(Listed in order of admission to membership. Bullets denote companies listed on the Tokyo Stock Exchange or a local stock exchange or trading over-the-counter.)

Figure 1. Overview of Member Companies of the NPS Research Association

million). Sales of these five companies alone total approximately ¥900 billion ($3.5 billion).

There is a long list of over 300 companies currently applying for membership, according to Mikiya Kinoshita, chief director of the NPS Research Association. When *Shukan Toyo Keizai*, the Japanese financial newspaper, carried a special report on NPS, the editors were deluged with telephone calls requesting information about membership. Some inquirers even visited the newspaper's office in Nihonbashi. Kinoshita reportedly received 200 to 300 additional membership applications after he revealed the membership figure of 300.

Toyo Keizai has reliable information on companies that will be admitted to membership in the near future. All of the companies are leaders in their respective industries and most are listed on the Tokyo Stock Exchange.

I mentioned earlier that NPS, as a corporate group, would probably become larger than Toyota. When you think about it, this is not all that difficult. For example, if 100 companies with annual sales of about ¥50 billion ($200 million) join NPS, the total annual sales would be ¥5 trillion ($20 billion). In 1986 alone, big companies such as Noritsu, manufacturer of gas water heaters; Kurinappu, manufacturer of bathroom cabinets; Shinto Kogyo, a foundry plant; Uni Charm, manufacturer of diapers and sanitary products; and Shin Nikkei, manufacturer of aluminum sash, did join NPS. Total 1986 sales of NPS member companies were ¥1.5 trillion ($7.5 billion). More big businesses were expected to join NPS during 1987, potentially doubling the combined total sales of NPS member companies.

Does the NPS Research Association have the ability and know-how to provide adequate leadership and guidance to many more companies than its current members? Although Kinoshita is confident that NPS can handle at least 300 companies, he acknowledges holding back on new admissions because present members fear that their addition may disrupt the present comfortable atmosphere. On the other hand, member companies themselves keep coming to Kinoshita requesting that specific companies be allowed to join.

In 1985, NPS employed 11 instructors — not a large number. Most of the instructors are former employees of the Toyota Motor Company or one of its affiliates. All of the instructors were taught Toyota's production methods either directly by Taiichi Ohno, widely acknowledged as the father of the kanban and Toyota production systems, or by Kikuo Suzumura, chairman of NPS's Implementation Committee, and all gained experience in teaching the method to others while employees of a Toyota group company.

Some say that an auto industry worker cannot understand the intricacies of the food, clothing, or housing industries. While understandable, this is not true. Whenever Taiichi Ohno meets Masahito Hoashi, president of Kibun, he asks, "Do you see now that making boiled-fish paste is no different from making cars?"

How can making boiled fish paste products be the same as producing cars? How can a modern plant for producing cars be the same as one for producing boiled-fish paste products? It does not seem possible. Yet NPS instructors can tell just by inspecting a plant what is wrong with it and how to correct its problems. They can identify the problems and start shop floor improvements all in the same day.

This happened not only at Kibun. At World, a leader in the apparel industry, NPS instructors were able to point out within hours of their arrival what was wrong with the production lines and their production method. Productivity increased significantly once their advice was implemented.

At any rate, before a company joins NPS, its top managers and production-level workers usually have a strong degree of pride in their existing production method, based on years of experience. That outsiders — former auto-industry people, for example — can just walk in, immediately understand what is happening, and correct any problems is greeted with skepticism.

NPS instructors, however, have a power of observation combined with an ability to perform that has impressed President Chiyoji Misawa of Misawa Homes, who admits, "I was never made so aware of the difference between those that can and those that can't. The NPS people can, and they are terrific."

The 11 instructors are also referred to as Implementation Committee Members. Kinoshita says that there are at least 200 individuals in the member companies — a number that is bound to increase — with ability comparable to the 11 instructors. This means that NPS has a talent pool to draw on to meet a potentially rapid increase in membership. Because of this resource pool, I believe that NPS will continue to accept new members and rapidly increase its influence.

A One-Industry, One-Company Organization

The greatest strength of the NPS Research Association lies in its strong solidarity and the mutual trust among its members. It is not just a study group. Members are independent companies bound by comradeship and a shared philosophy. This comradeship exists not only among the presidents of the member companies but extends down to the lowest-level employees and part-time workers. Workers attend gatherings sponsored by their own company to foster friendship among themselves, to talk about their company and NPS "lingo," and to learn about the other NPS companies.

The NPS network is spreading — and I believe that the solidarity within the network may be stronger than that among any other corporate group. The Matsushita group is permeated with the so-called Matsushita-ism developed by Konosuke Matsushita. However, there is no denying that Matsushita Electric Industrial, the nucleus of the group, has now become too large and inflexible. I do not think that there are study groups — programs aimed at fostering interaction among the employees of the different group companies — at Matsushita that encompass even the lowest-level employees.

The NPS group has another advantage. Its members represent different industries. Members of the Matsushita or Toyota groups are mainly from the same industry, be it electrical or automotive. In addition, these established groups rely heavily on exports — Matsushita Electric's amount to nearly 40 percent and Toyota's to nearly 50 percent of gross sales. It is quite possible, for example, for growing friction over trade or a steep rise in the value of the yen to transform into a weakness what has previously been a strength.

Many different industries are represented in the NPS group due to its policy of "one industry, one company." With a one company per industry organization, a difficulty experienced by one firm can be offset by the success of another so that the group as a whole will remain well balanced and healthy. The group has a strength that comes with flexibility. A high level of self-sufficiency is another strength made possible among the member companies. In difficult times, NPS members can help one another.

The NPS Research Association is now beginning to shed its veil of mystery by aggressively publicizing itself to forestall unwarranted misunderstandings, rumors, and biases. It should be remembered, however, that the existence of NPS went unnoticed for a long time because of the "code of silence" that formerly bound the members. According to Hirotoshi Hatasaki, president of World, there was a rule that talking about NPS to outsiders constituted grounds for termination of membership. Some member companies had gone so far as to issue a "gag rule" forbidding employees to discuss their NPS membership with outsiders.

No secret, however, can be kept forever. A company has not only its own employees, perhaps numbering in the thousands, but also part-time workers and helpers. One cannot monitor all their conversations all the time. People like to talk about what is happening at their company and sometimes workers complain, for example, about NPS after work at a bar.

It is true that strong opposition to NPS exists within some of the member companies. Some people have even quit their jobs because they could not accept NPS's way of doing things. It would not be surprising to hear criticism from those who have left a company because of differences over NPS. They may allege that NPS will harm or is planning to take over the company or that the workers are being worked too hard.

There are also cases in which NPS has so greatly improved a company's business that its top executives cannot refrain from talking about it despite the gag rule. This is how Noboru Kawasaki, president of Kawasaki Electric, manufacturer of switchboards and other electrical equipment, found out about NPS. According to Kawasaki, his good friend Tsutomu Ihara, president of Ihara Koatsu Tsugite Kogyo, was concerned about Kawasaki Electric's perilous financial condition. He told Kawasaki that he knew a consultant who could quickly extract any company from financial difficulty and that his own company had used that consultant for its own rescue.

Ihara says that having seen his own company pulled safely back from the brink of bankruptcy, he could not bear to watch Kawasaki worry about his company. After describing NPS to Kawasaki, Ihara was worried that his own company's membership might be cancelled and he hesitated to ask Director Kinoshita to take a look at Kawasaki Electric. Ihara noted, however, that although he had thus broken a rule of membership, the so-called statute of limitations had already expired.

Most of the member companies have outstanding bank loans. If bank officials should ask how the business had been turned around so quickly, it would be difficult for them not to discuss NPS. For the sake of good long-term relations, it is prudent for company executives to keep bank officials posted on some of their management efforts. If a company officer describes to a bank official how improving the production line in such and such a way has greatly increased productivity, the bank official before long will want to take a look at the plant.

But the main reason that Kinoshita and others at NPS decided to go public was that they feared the spread of unfounded rumors and misunderstandings.

Handing the NPS Philosophy Down to Posterity

Kinoshita explains the reason for publicizing the existence of NPS as follows:

> In the beginning, there was no need for the public to know about our existence. We did not want unnecessary sensationalism. However, their businesses improved, members told us that they were finding it difficult to come up with plausible explanations. We also became aware that some people were making irresponsible statements about us. We ourselves can put up with rumors — but we cannot tolerate, for example, having the workers of member companies being disturbed by such rumors. So, from about the spring of 1985, we have permitted limited disclosure concerning NPS.

The underground rumors spreading about NPS were indeed not very flattering. As I mentioned earlier, workers who had to quit their jobs after years of service because of the changes introduced by NPS naturally spread all kinds of derogatory information about the organization. Personal attacks were also directed against Kinoshita and others who had implemented NPS methods. Some even characterized NPS as a mysterious organization whose member companies hold each others' stocks and amass enormous profits through insider trading. Such stories were being disseminated as true.

Representatives of some companies that were denied membership spitefully spread reports that NPS's annual consulting fee was ¥ 300-400 million ($1.2-1.6 million), a gross exaggeration.

For protection against unfounded criticism and malicious gossip, NPS top management concluded that it was necessary to give the public some true facts concerning the purposes and philosophy of the NPS Research Association.

The NPS Research Association, headed by Mikiya Kinoshita, then president of Ushio Electric, was established in January 1980, by the presidents of five companies: Oiresu, Kibun, Ogura Hoseki Seiki Kogyo, Ikuyo, and Yoga Seiko Sha. Yokogawa Electric, Skylark, and others joined later. As of 1985, the membership numbered 29 companies.

A company cannot become a member by simply paying the membership dues. First of all, there is the rule that each industry will be represented by only one company. The reason is that the NPS Research Association is meant to be a forum for the frank exchange of experiences, both good and bad, among members who are bound by the same philosophy and a spirit of comradeship. It is feared that the presence of several companies from the same industry would hamper such frank discussion. With companies belonging to different industries, there is no danger that vital secrets will be stolen when a plant is opened up for a tour of inspection or when openly discussing what one is trying to accomplish.

With companies from different industries, candid disclosure is easier, and such openness may result in better suggestions. A close relationship is therefore easier to establish. These are some of the reasons that NPS admits membership to only one company from each industry. This policy may appear exclusionary and unnecessarily secretive to others.

Does NPS membership require payment of an exorbitant membership fee? I asked Chiyoji Misawa, a relatively new member at that time, about this. Misawa replied: "I was surprised. I was expecting to pay a very high membership fee, but the actual fee is virtually zero. NPS does not seek anything in return for membership." Noboru Kawasaki says, "We have been a member for two years — since January 1983. However, they still won't accept any membership fee from us. We have offered to pay but they say that we are still only a junior member, like a pre-school child in a kindergarten. They insist we still don't have to pay." Kawasaki Electric's main plant is in Yamagata, an area famous for its many hot springs. None of the NPS instructors who have come to Yamagata have even so much as hinted that they would like to spend the night at one of those resorts. Once they arrive at the plant, they are quick to inspect it, make suggestions for improvement, and then depart the area, on the last flight out, if necessary.

Refuting rumors about high membership fees, Kinoshita states:

> Reports of membership dues of some ¥400 million ($1.6 million) per company are totally unfounded. We only want to offer our services to companies that share our philosophy and will cooperate to pass along our philosophy to posterity. The people at NPS are not concerned about money. We shun offers of payment, but members keep insisting. So, like wandering monks, when we sometimes do accept payment, it is looked upon as alms.

Depending on the size of the company, members are required to pay a monthly fee of ¥500,000 ($2,000), ¥800,000 ($3,200), or ¥1,200,000 ($4,800). There are no other charges of any kind.

However, companies admitted to membership in NPS are required to buy shares in a company called MIP ("Mutual Identity and Prosperity"), a holding company for NPS. Mikiya

Kinoshita is also president of MIP. A company must invest either ¥ 3 million ($12,000) or ¥ 6 million ($24,000) to become a stockholder. However, the companies are allowed to buy the shares whenever they choose and are not pressured. Kinoshita explains: "MIP is formed by and belongs to the members of NPS. MIP foots the bill for expenses incurred by members of the Implementation Committee during the period of a company's application for membership in NPS and its formal admission. That is all."

A Divinely Inspired Group?

It is still astounding to note the improvements experienced by the member companies of NPS. One reason that NPS is becoming better known to the public is that most of the member companies have attained a performance level that gives them the confidence to weather any criticism levied at them by the public.

Actually, there are numerous examples of NPS member companies dramatically improving their business in a short period of time, or of companies once considered moribund returning to life and vigor with renewed prospects for a bright future. Of course, there are companies such as Akai Electric that are still facing difficulties, but recovery cannot occur until all the infection has been rooted out.

The improvement achieved by the member companies becomes obvious when one looks at the *Kaisha Shikiho* [a quarterly handbook that provides condensed financial data on major Japanese corporations] published by Toyo Keizai. For example, Yokogawa Hokushin Electric, one of the oldest members of NPS, achieved a 43 percent increase in ordinary profits for the period ending March 1985 as compared with the previous period despite being burdened by its merger with Hokushin Denki in April 1983. Skylark achieved a 16 percent increase in ordinary profits for the period ending December 1984 as compared to the previous period. Nipponcoinco achieved a 71 percent increase in ordinary profits for the period ending July 1984 over the previous period. Okamoto Machine Tool Works achieved a 134 percent increase, Bando Chemical Industries a 54 percent increase, and Shigetsu Denki a 76 percent increase in their ordinary profits. In fact, profits have increased for most NPS companies.

Companies such as Kawasaki Denki, Nozawa, Hokuetsu Kogyo (which is listed on a local stock exchange), and Ihara Koatsu Tsugite (traded over the counter) have recovered quickly from deep financial trouble. According to its president, Kosuke Asano, Nippon Light Metal, which as the victim of a structural recession was forced to sell its headquarters in the Ginza, is now staying in the black month after month.

Among unlisted companies, World, the largest apparel manufacturer, achieved an annual ordinary profit of ¥22.8 billion ($90 million) despite the poor performance of other apparel manufacturers. There are many small companies that are doing very well.

What, then, is this NPS Research Association that has succeeded so quickly in improving the business of its member companies? Some people view the NPS group as some sort of divinely inspired cult.

To those who do not understand NPS, its philosophy and principles may indeed appear cultlike. This is understandable, considering that NPS rejects what 99 percent of the people accept as good and teaches that one must cast aside some aspects of common sense. Naturally, some people react negatively to NPS. It is impossible for some people to discard what they have been taught as good and what they sincerely believe to be good. Because they cannot accept NPS, they disparage it as being cultlike, and refuse to change their old belief structure. It is easy to dismiss NPS as a cultlike organization, as heretical, or as wrong-headed consultants. The fact remains, however, that the number of companies that — having witnessed achieved results — are now willing to learn from NPS, is rapidly increasing.

———

CHAPTER TWO

Keeping Up with Changing Times

J APAN'S period of rapid economic growth has ended. It is
now the age of stable, slow growth. The Japanese economy
will probably never be as vigorous and dynamic as it was during
the high-growth period. Japan has the second largest economy in the free world after the United States. An island nation
in the Far East, without natural resources and handicapped by
defeat in a major war, Japan has rebounded magnificently
thanks to the efforts and diligence of its people. In the eyes of
other advanced nations, the economic recovery of Japan is
nothing short of a miracle.

There is, however, no guarantee that the Japanese economy
will continue to prosper indefinitely. Of course, there is no
need to worry that it will suddenly fall flat on its face, reverse
past trends, and enter a hopelessly dismal state. The most
likely scenario is for the economy to keep growing with minor
ripples of recession and boom.

Even though the Japanese national economy may grow
gradually with occasional recessions, individual industries
and companies will not all follow the same path. The difference between industries and companies that grow and those
that fail will probably become more pronounced.

During the period when Japan suffered from a lack of foreign currency, export industries were treasured. Companies that increased the country's exports received a special award from the Ministry of International Trade and Industry (MITI). The situation is completely different today. Foreign countries now consider Japan's export industries a source of trade friction, and even MITI — previously the unquestioning proponent of exports — is calling for self-restraint by Japan's exporters.

The Japanese home appliance and automobile industries, previously much praised for their exports, are now the target of criticism. Pressure from abroad to restrict exports is colliding head-on with the growth of these industries as the domestic market becomes saturated. The stronger home appliance and automobile manufacturers are avoiding the problems of trade friction and import restrictions by overseas production and other means. However, almost all of these measures, including overseas production, are measures of last resort.

It is common knowledge that the period of high growth for the Japanese economy is over. The domestic market is saturated, and there is no assurance that the export market will expand.

Nevertheless, most companies still believe in mass production and mass sales. Many companies say that they intend to switch from relatively undiversified high-volume production to highly diversified low-volume production. And there is evidence that companies are expanding their product diversity to meet the diversifying needs of consumers. However, even though their intentions of increasing their product diversity and market share are well thought out, companies persist in using methods based on mass production even as they talk about highly diversified low-volume production. Their views on inventory, for example, are highly suspect.

Many companies boast that their production quantity per product is getting smaller and that their production diversity is increasing. However, in most cases the drop in production quantity per product occurred not because they had planned and intended it but because poor sales had forced them to reduce production. There is a big difference between low-volume production based on efforts to produce only what can be sold and low-volume production that occurs unintentionally because of poor sales. In the former case, production is based on the amount that *can be sold*; in the latter, production is based on the amount that is *expected* to be sold. When only what can be sold is produced, there is no merchandise left over. On the other hand, when production is based on hunch, underproduction occurs when products sell better than expected, and inventories accumulate when the products do not sell well.

Corporate Traps

Manufacturers find it truly annoying when there are not enough products to meet the orders. When a manufacturer engages in highly diversified low-volume production and produces a limited amount when sales are unexpectedly good, the manufacturer feels that it has suffered a loss. This forgone opportunity to sell what could have been sold is called opportunity loss.

To any company, the fish that gets away looks biggest. If a company pursues low-volume production and an opportunity loss occurs, the salespeople will probably rant and rave, demanding to know why more products were not produced. If a competitor with a similar product succeeds in expanding sales, the company may feel threatened by the loss of market share. As a result, it may place paramount importance on securing the market share by producing a surplus to meet any unexpectedly high demand. Those responsible for making production and sales plans may think: "Our products aren't going to rot or spoil because what we produce will eventually be sold. Producing a surplus will provide the benefit of cost reduction through mass production. A cost reduction will allow us to reduce our price, making us more competitive. It's okay to produce a surplus — as long as we motivate our sales force to sell what is produced."

There is a hidden pitfall. Many companies cannot shed the belief that when a surplus is produced, it will be sold sooner or later. Except for the owner, all employees of a Japanese company, including most presidents and directors, are hired hands. Hired employees may be diligent and hard working, but they also tend to be irresponsible. They like to blame others for what they should have done. They make excuses, such as "He told me to" or "It's always been this way," to avoid responsibility. If products remain unsold, they will look for excuses rather than admit their mistake.

This criticism applies equally to most company owners as well. Many act important but lack an independent decision-making ability, prefering to serve their term, avoid trouble, and retire with a large pension. They don't want to rock the boat.

To sum up, it is easy to criticize when there are not enough products to sell and easy to blame someone else when surplus products remain unsold. At many companies, the once intended low-volume production has regressed to medium or even high volume.

Many companies claim highly diversified, small-lot production as their policy but feel insecure when they do not have some inventory on hand. They are obsessed with avoiding opportunity loss. This creates a tolerance for inventory. Because a company wants to respond immediately to customer demand, it builds up an inventory of many types of goods. The inventory increases both in width (product types) and depth (quantity). The product of the width multiplied by the depth is inventory volume, which becomes huge.

If a company's inventory and debts are growing rapidly despite a slow increase in sales, that company is producing on the basis of *expected sales* and is insensitive to the rising volume of unsold products even if professing to believe in highly diversified low-volume production.

The Fallacy of Appropriate Inventory

Every company owner knows how dangerous excessive inventory can be. There are numerous examples of companies getting into trouble and even going bankrupt because of excessive inventory. However, company owners who shudder at the thought of excessive inventory do not think twice about maintaining "appropriate inventory." If told that appropriate inventory is equal to one month's sales, they accept that figure unquestioningly. Frequently it is only when significant funds become tied up in several months' worth of inventory that a company owner becomes aware of the amount of inventory. But it is very difficult to reduce inventory once that stage is reached. For one thing, most of the product inventory is composed of unsold goods that are worth next to nothing. Company owners are loath to write off the inventory because this creates a book loss, indicating a weakened financial condition.

"Appropriate inventory" sounds good. The opposite of "appropriate" is "*in*appropriate." The words "appropriate" and "inappropriate" are interchangeable with "success" and "failure." Inventory in excess of the appropriate amount is considered inappropriate, that is, excessive. But what is appropriate inventory? The basis for appropriateness frequently is experience. But the experience gained during the period of high economic growth may not be directly applicable in a period of low, stable economic growth. This is the first problem.

Why is inventory necessary in the first place? And how can any given level of inventory be called appropriate? Why don't people realize that maintaining no inventory at all can make a company more agile?

NPS does not tolerate inventory, but considers it a source of evil. This is in contrast to the generally accepted notion of appropriate inventory. Is it NPS or the general public that is mistaken? The answer has already been given.

When Kikuo Suzumura visited the main plant of a company seeking NPS membership, he rebuked the company president and plant executives the moment he set foot in their raw materials warehouse. Weighing more than 220 pounds, Suzumura looks formidable. When he says in his Mikawa dialect: "What's the matter with you?" most people are terrified. Suzumura told the company executives to bring out all the money in the company safe and in their wallets.

The company president, the plant manager, and the other plant executives did as they were told. Suzumura told the plant manager and the manager of the raw materials section to tape the ¥10,000 notes (worth about $40 in 1985) to the boxes of raw materials piled high in the warehouse. After the two had taped several notes to the boxes, Suzumura said:

> Compare the cash that is here and these piles of raw materials. The cash in the safe is peanuts. What about this inventory? Is this all free? With cash, you keep what you need for the day in the safe and deposit the remainder at a bank. But this inventory keeps increasing every day. You don't think inventory is money? Inventory *is* money. If inventory is so important you have to store it in a warehouse, why aren't you paid your salaries with inventory, instead of cash?

Suzumura's unique logic convinced the plant personnel that inventory ties up funds and decreases a company's efficiency.

The following happened at a different company when its president said with pride: "This is the newest three-dimensional warehouse. We can retrieve any material stored anywhere in the warehouse just by throwing a switch. With the new warehouse, we have dramatically reduced labor costs." Suzumura asked the company president to take the elevator with him to the top of the warehouse. At the top, with the puzzled president in tow, Suzumura instructed him: "Look down. How do you feel?" The company president replied: "It's so high it's almost scary." Suzumura answered: "Scared? What's scary? You are the one who built this. You'd be the only one killed if you fell from here. The people who are really scared are the employees who work for a company that built such a stupid thing and is facing possible bankruptcy. You tie up your money and your products, you threaten your company with bankruptcy, and still you act like a big boss. I don't understand." This episode is another illustration of NPS's philosophy that inventory is evil.

Suzumura has said: "I would like to meet the stupid scholar who coined the phrase 'inventory investment.' How can inventory be an investment? Inventory only makes a company inflexible. If someone says having inventory makes him feel secure, I say, 'Go ahead. You're on your own.'"

Ohno's Departure from Toyota

While at Toyota, Kikuo Suzumura was known throughout the auto industry for his astute management. Suzumura was the top disciple of Taiichi Ohno whom he addressed affectionately with great respect as *oyaji* [a term of endearment that literally means "father" or "boss"]. Suzumura left his post as senior inspector of Toyota Motor's Production Management Department in 1978, when Ohno left his job as a Toyota vice-president. Suzumura felt no further attachment to Toyota after Taiichi Ohno's departure.

Ohno and Suzumura had a devotion to Toyota that was probably second to no one's. Without such devotion, it would have been impossible to overcome the many difficulties in developing the Toyota production system, a production method without any counterpart in the world. Ohno and Suzumura must have expended tremendous effort in overcoming the myriad misunderstandings, biased views, and obstacles while developing the Toyota production system with its emphasis on the total elimination of waste.

According to industry sources, several events led to their departure from Toyota. Until the stockholders' meeting in September 1978, the board of directors of Toyota Motor consisted of Chairman Shoichi Saito, President Eiji Toyoda, Vice-president Shoichiro Toyoda, Vice-president Taiichi Ohno, and Vice-president Masaya Hanai. Taiichi Ohno and Masaya Hanai were widely known to be not only business rivals, but personal enemies as well. After the stockholders' meeting, a change in personnel took place: the board of directors became Chairman Masaya Hanai, President Eiji Toyoda, Vice-president Shoichiro Toyoda, Vice-president Hidetaro Mori, and Vice-president Shigenobu Yamamoto. In other words, Hanai became chairman of Toyota while Ohno was bumped from the board.

This incensed Ohno. Hanai had come up through the accounting side of the firm, following the footsteps of the late Taizo Ishida who was known as Toyota's "manager of managers." As far as Ohno was concerned, Toyota's present eminence as a company that even Ford and General Motors were willing to learn from resulted not from Toyota's solid accounting practices, but from the efforts made by the production, marketing, and sales departments.

Toyota is sometimes referred to as the "Toyota Bank" because of its robust financial condition. But, as far as Ohno was concerned, the financial strength came about because cars were produced and sold, not because accounting had come up with the money. The accounting departments had just wisely managed the funds. Suzumura, after sharing many difficulties and successes with Ohno, was disillusioned by the restructuring, which gave priority not to the people who toiled on the production floors, but to staff managers who lounged comfortably in their three-piece suits.

It is also said that Ohno and Hanai clashed over the handling of overseas production and the merger between Toyota's two independent branches, Toyota Jiko (production) and Toyota Jihan (sales), which finally took place in July 1982. There is no doubt that a rising concern over trade friction had led Toyota Motor to become increasingly convinced during the period from the late 1970s to the early 1980s that some form of domestic production within the United States would eventually be necessary.

Ohno and Hanai clashed head-on over what form this American production operation should take. Hanai said an independent venture in the United States would cost too much and therefore be too risky. He maintained that forming a partnership with General Motors would reduce the required investment, lessen the discomfort that American workers might feel in working for a Japanese firm, and otherwise smooth Toyota's way in the United States. Hanai wanted to enjoy the fruits of overseas production while paying as little as possible for it — a typical accountant's view.

Ohno's views were the opposite. He maintained that if Toyota's entry into the United States was inevitable, Toyota should do it on its own. Understandably, Ohno maintained that the investment should be held to a minimum, and that production should be started on a small scale and then expanded if things went well. It is said that Ohno was adamant in his view that Toyota should go it alone, because a partnership with General Motors would mean exposing everything about the Toyota production system. He believed that placing this knowledge in the hands of an American automobile producer would return to haunt Toyota in the future.

Ohno is said to have opposed the merger between Toyota Jiko and Toyota Jihan while Hanai supported it. In theory, bringing the production and sales arms together would enable the market needs — discovered by sales — to be relayed quickly to production. Production could then be tailored to the actual market demands. This practice of bringing production and sales together to quicken response to the market is sometimes referred to as integration of production and sales.

It is widely acknowledged that a major Toyota strength lay in the fact that production and sales were independent of each other. The two separate companies were like two wheels sharing a common axis and driving the entire Toyota group forward. Nissan Motor, for example, had an integrated production and sales structure, and was not necessarily more responsive to market trends than Toyota. Ohno reportedly believed that Toyota Jihan's independent stability allowed Toyota Jiko to concentrate on production and thereby create a solid financial foundation for the entire group.

Toyota rejected Ohno's viewpoint. It selected General Motors as its partner in starting U.S. production, and merged its sales and production arms. Only history will tell conclusively whether Toyota made the right move in forming a partnership with General Motors.

Obsessed with Chasing Toyota

Toyota Motor is not the subject of this book. My intention is simply to impress upon the reader how Taiichi Ohno and Kikuo Suzumura became the central members of the NPS Research Association and why they are so devoted to helping its member companies. It may be too cynical to say that Ohno and his disciple Suzumura left Toyota because Hanai became chairman. I cannot help feeling that their intention now is to further develop the Toyota production system and the kanban method, which they created with the help of others, and to pass their philosophy on to posterity. Mikiya Kinoshita says

Ohno goes from one company to another, without greed, like a wandering monk.

I wrote earlier that NPS would become a corporate group that surpasses Toyota in 10 or 15 years. When I think about the bitter mortification Ohno and Suzumura must have felt in having to leave Toyota, I can sense the kind of determination they must have — perhaps unconsciously — to surpass Toyota during their lifetimes.

CHAPTER THREE

The Difference between the NPS Method and the Toyota Method

W HEN people hear that the central figures of NPS are Taiichi Ohno and Kikuo Suzumura, both former employees of Toyota, and Mikiya Kinoshita, the former president of Ushio Electric who learned the Toyota production system from Ohno and implemented it to resurrect his company, they may think that NPS teaches the Toyota production system or the zero-inventory method that originated at Toyota. Some even feel that NPS should call itself the Toyota production system or the kanban method instead of the New Production System.

However, Ohno and Suzumura are not inspired by Toyota, and they say the Toyota production system and kanban method apply only to Toyota. Ohno, in fact, says nothing more can be learned from Toyota's production methods. He claims that Toyota's present system is quite different from what Suzumura or he directed on Toyota's production floors.

Before Nippon Light Metal became a member of NPS, Masaomi Ueda, a vice-president who was not well acquainted with NPS's philosophy, asked Kinoshita to show him one of Toyota's plants. Kinoshita said: "It is useless to inspect a Toyota plant because nothing is to be learned there. A better example is Kanto Auto Works, whose Yokosuka plant boasts the highest productivity in the world."

From Type III to Type II Manufacturing

Why does Kinoshita say nothing is to be learned from Toyota? According to Suzumura: "NPS's approach is more advanced than Toyota's. For example, unlike NPS, Toyota has not realized that Type II production is more efficient than Type III production." Figure 2 illustrates the three types of production.

Suzumura uses a description of three systems of sushi preparation to explain what he means: The sushi made for sale at supermarkets is mass-produced in advance according to ex-

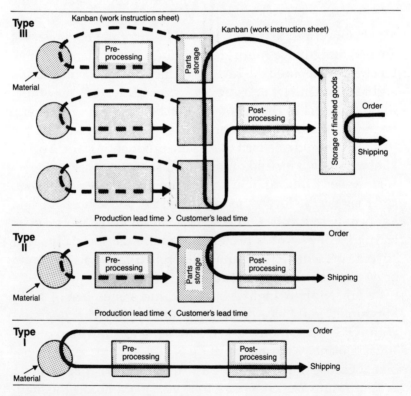

Figure 2. Type I, II, and III Production

pected sales. At Kozo Sushi (a popular low-price chain restaurant), sushi is partially assembled in advance for fast service to customers, then completed to order. This is Type III production. At a sit-down sushi restaurant, the fish is sliced, the rice shaped, and the sushi assembled after the customer places an order. This is Type II production; it is superior to Type III in providing fresher food for the customer as well as eliminating the waste of storing varieties of made-up sushi that customers aren't ordering that day.

Suzumura says: "During our days at Toyota — a period of slow economic growth in Japan — Toyota led the manufacturing sector using Type III production. We could not escape the waste of storing finished goods. From our efforts to eliminate this step, Type II production evolved."

Changes are occurring at Toyota. Formerly the company adhered unwaveringly to the just-in-time system, an approach based on the idea of maintaining zero inventory. However, since a major transportation accident that blocked the Nippon Zaka Tunnel and left the company temporarily without necessary components, Toyota has reportedly been carrying from a half-day's to a full day's inventory. This policy is utterly contrary to the Toyota zero-inventory method. Perhaps this is one of the changes that prompted Ohno and Suzumura to say that the present Toyota production system is different from the one they had previously known.

An accident of the magnitude of the Nippon Zaka Tunnel disaster probably occurs no more frequently than once every ten years. Hence, NPS considers it unnecessary to behave as if such an accident occurs often. Maintaining enough inventory to ensure a steady supply of parts in case of another such accident is therefore inappropriate. According to news reports, Toyota is also changing the way it invests in plants and equipment. Instead of maintaining a steady, even level of investment, the company now appears to be making lump sum investments of several tens of billions of yen (approximately $40 million dollars) at a time. This investment style is another difference between the present Toyota system and that of the days when Ohno and Suzumura worked there.

The NPS Mission: Improving Corporate Efficiency

Kinoshita and Suzumura say that NPS is concerned not only with production but with the efficient operation of the entire corporation. They say this makes the NPS approach completely different from Toyota's production system or kanban method.

Indeed, NPS is concerned not only with the rationalization of production. Its goal is to spread the NPS philosophy throughout the entire company, starting with the company president. According to Kinoshita, NPS's basic philosophy — eliminating all waste from company management — involves two approaches. The first is to seek production technology that allows minimal use of equipment and labor in producing defect-free goods, in the shortest possible time, with the least amount of unfinished goods left over.

The second approach is to regard as waste any element that does not contribute to meeting the quality, price, or delivery deadline required by the users, and to strive to eliminate such waste through the concerted effort of all sections of the company, including top management, research and development, distribution, and production-floor workers.

CPAs and Banks: Unnecessary Evils

One thing that shows NPS's concern with more than just production is Kinoshita's condemnation of certified public accountants (CPAs). Corporate managers usually refrain from criticizing CPAs because they do not want them commenting unfavorably about them in their audit reports. It is rare to hear CPAs condemned as an unnecessary evil, but Kinoshita does so openly. He maintains:

It is presumptuous for someone who knows little about running a company to audit that company's books. It is inexcusable for such a person to stop production or close down a warehouse and halt the movement of goods just so he or she can check the inventory. It may be tolerable to do this on a holiday, but to do it on a weekday is quite unacceptable. We pay CPAs very well, but can you name a single CPA who can offer advice that actually improves corporate performance? Everybody knows that inventory is a burden for a company. Then, why don't CPAs advise companies to eliminate inventory? Maybe the reason is that counting inventories gives CPAs something to do. We advise NPS member companies to get rid of any useless CPAs. When a company has something to hide from the CPAs, management is careful to say nothing to irritate them, hoping that this will keep them from hunting for faults. But, since members of the NPS group have nothing to hide, they have no need to kowtow to CPAs.

NPS believes that CPAs who are not concerned with eliminating inventory — a factor that raises a company's operating costs — are unnecessary and wasteful.

Banks are not spared either. In Japan, banks frequently send employees to borrower companies, usually as members of the board of directors or in some other high position, to protect the bank's security interest. Suzumura says:

Banks are like people who stick a straw into a watermelon and suck out all the juice. When they are through, all that remains is the rind. There's nothing left to eat when you cut it open. Look, there are many firms with a good operating profit that becomes marginal or even turns into a loss when interest is paid to the banks. It's as if we're working for the banks. Employees spend their valuable time working for their company, but the profits go to the banks. This is incredible. The management borrowing the money is, of course, not blameless, but the banks are worse.

Kinoshita agrees and makes clear that he is not going to allow banks to run the companies:

Banks survive by sucking the lifeblood of corporations. They are terrible. They not only charge high interest but place their own people on the staffs of the borrowing companies. These people usually contribute nothing but act as watchdogs. They're all like that. They think they can do anything they want to the company. It really makes me angry. Once we get enough clout, we'll repay all the loans and send the bank people back to their banks.

Kinoshita recognizes that it is sometimes necessary to borrow from banks. When he heard that a bank had refused to lend operating capital to NPS member Kawasaki Electric because of poor performance, he met with the bank president and persuaded him to make the loan at a fairly low interest rate. According to Noboru Kawasaki, president of Kawasaki Electric, which was near bankruptcy as a result of massive losses: "Kinoshita went to see Mamoru Sakai, president of the Long-Term Credit Bank of Japan, Kawasaki Electric's main bank, and requested that Kawasaki Electric be lent the funds. He guaranteed that he would personally see to it that the company got back on its feet."

Companies cannot exist without funds. At times, it may be necessary to borrow money. However, interest must be paid for the borrowed money. NPS instructs its member companies to manage the company so that it is not necessary to borrow money at high interest rates.

Increasing Productivity throughout the Company

Another clue that NPS is concerned with more than production management is evident in its instruction that monthly accounts be settled quickly. Kinoshita says:

> Why is every company so slow in closing its monthly accounts? I can understand it taking a week or ten days to close the monthly accounts, but it takes one to two months to do this with almost every company. If we keep track of market trends and our daily revenues and expenditures, we should be able to close the monthly accounts by the first day of the following month. But accountants don't keep track of accounts on a day-by-day basis. Instead they try to do everything at once, and they have to stay up all night doing this. If they did their job every day, there would be no need for working overtime. They talk about 'improving production-floor productivity,' but they don't even know what they themselves are supposed to do everyday. How can we plan future production or sales when it takes one or two months to close the monthly accounts? This indicates management without direction.

Kinoshita instructs accounting departments to spread out their work load and adhere to the just-in-time philosophy.

Sales departments, too, come in for criticism. According to Suzumura:

> Sales departments make a fuss about production not meeting delivery deadlines. My opinion is that those in sales must change their views. Have you ever noticed that the salespeople at almost every company bring in most of their orders at the end of the month or accounting period? They don't make many sales early in the month. Orders start coming in around the tenth of the month, and they try to meet their monthly quota during its last

few days. This puts excessive strain on production, which is told to meet the deadlines.

But, how can you meet deadlines when you are always forced to bite off more than you can chew? In order to meet the last-minute production schedules imposed by sales, we must muster the equipment, materials, and labor normally needed only for peak loads. This is foolish. Sales departments must stop flooding production with orders at the end of the month. Sales must try to bring in a constant daily volume of orders and provide production with information on orders as soon as possible. But the truth is that many salesmen go to pachinko [a pinball-type game] parlors or to coffee shops and waste their time when they leave the company in the morning.

These practices must stop at once. It is not difficult. All it takes is to require every salesman to write down who he is seeing, at what time, and when he will return, and to post this information in a visible place. Every now and then, you have somebody call the client to verify that the salesman is where he says he will be. If you do this once or twice, you'll put an end to the practice of loafing on the job. Companies must not be preoccupied with the productivity of only the production departments. An increase in productivity in one area can be easily offset by a decrease in productivity in another. The most important thing is to increase the overall productivity of the entire company.

Starting a Distribution Network

Another noteworthy development is the distribution system developed by NPS members for their own use. NPS is pushing the just-in-time philosophy to the utmost by developing its own transportation network for linking the manufacturers of parts and material with the processors, the assemblers, and the users.

Following a six-month study, NPS joint transportation network — extending 1200 kilometers between Toyota and Morioka and linking three plants belonging to Yokogawa Hokushin Electric, Nippon Atsudenki, and Nipponcoinco — went into operation in June 1985. Ten-ton trucks, making two trips per day between Tokyo and Morioka on a precise schedule, link the parts manufacturers, the parts assemblers, and the users.

This transportation link marks the beginning of the rationalization of distribution by tailoring distribution on plant's daily production. The idea is to schedule the pickup of items so that each truck spends the shortest possible time at any one place. Suzumura had long maintained that physical distribution is actually physical stagnation. The objective was to correct this situation. NPS plans to expand the Tohoku route (Tokyo to Morioka) by linking it to the Tokaido route (Tokyo to Osaka) in September. Other regional links are planned.

Keizo Kobayashi, manager of the NPS Promotion Department, says the benefits of precision distribution are already evident: "Goods shipped out twice a week means an inventory period of three to four days. Shipping goods twice a day drastically reduces the inventory of semifinished goods. Transportation costs also decrease slightly."

Transporting a large amount at a time reduces the transportation cost per item. However, when you consider the departure and arrival times, overall costs may become very high. NPS has chosen routes designed to cut transportation costs by reducing the amount of goods moved each time. This graphically illustrates that NPS is concerned not only with what happens inside the plants but with what happens between them.

PART TWO

Case Studies of
Member Companies

CHAPTER FOUR

Kawasaki Electric:
A Committed President Saves His Company

*I*T WAS in closing the books for the period ending March 1982 that Noboru Kawasaki, president of Kawasaki Electric, realized with fear that his company might go bankrupt. Noboru Kawasaki was a hard-nosed competitor. He was an optimist, but when the books showed that a loss and a reduction in the dividends were unavoidable, he saw dark days ahead.

In May 1982, Tsutomu Ihara, president of Ihara Koatsu Tsugite Kogyo, a leading manufacturer of high-pressure couplings, said words that sounded heaven-sent to Kawasaki, who had been worrying about his company without anyone to talk to. Ihara said: "There is a consultant group that can turn a failing company into an industry leader and rid its management of debt. We have joined that group and are working on changing our corporate environment."

Kawasaki did not believe his words immediately, and said: "A second-generation president like me tends not to believe in such things. I have hired my share of consultants, but all they did was take hundreds of millions of yen from me. Mr. Ihara, such a thing is a waste. There's no magic potion in this world." Ihara replied: "I'm also a second-generation president. I've made many mistakes. But this group is for real."

With his company facing imminent bankruptcy, Kawasaki was willing to grab at any straw and decided to take a gamble on the consultant group. When Kawasaki asked Ihara to introduce him, however, Ihara became less enthusiastic and said that not just anyone could join the group; the group was secret and Ihara would be expelled if it became known that he had talked about the group to a nonmember.

This further piqued Kawasaki's interest. He became impatient. He visited Ihara many times, each time asking him for his cooperation. Each rebuff by Ihara reinforced Kawasaki's belief that the only way to restore his company was to join this group. Every time Ihara said that Kawasaki's company, being a listed company, would never go bankrupt, Kawasaki responded by saying that any company, whether listed or not, could go bankrupt. Kawasaki patiently kept asking for Ihara's cooperation.

After this had gone on for some time, Kawasaki received a telephone call from Ihara. Ihara asked him if he was still interested in joining the group. Kawasaki reminded Ihara that he had been pleading with him since May for an introduction. Ihara then said that the director of the group was interested in meeting Kawasaki and asked Kawasaki to bring a financial statement for the last three years and a brief history of the company. Ihara said that he would submit the papers to the group.

Ihara told Kawasaki to wait, that the group would get in touch with him. One day Kawasaki was told to come, by himself, to the NPS Research Association's office in Tokyo's Ginza district. He still remembers the time and day. The appointment was for 3:30 p.m., October 12, 1982 — the day he turned 42, traditionally considered to be an unlucky age for Japanese men. He remembers heading for the office with feelings of both hope and trepidation.

"I Will Speak Only to the President"

Kawasaki met Mikiya Kinoshita for the first time. Kinoshita went directly to the heart of the matter and said: "Your company will probably go bankrupt. I looked at the closing accounts for the last three periods. Your company is almost hopeless. Do you know that?" Kawasaki responded: "I know that. That's why I'm here." Kinoshita asked: "How long have you been president?" Kawasaki answered: "It's been exactly eight years since my father passed away." Kinoshita said: "I'm amazed that the company has lasted so long with such a stupid president."

Kawasaki recalls fondly that Kinoshita called him stupid about 25 times during the meeting, which lasted from 3:30 to about 8:30 at night. Kawasaki says: "I've been called 'stupid' by my father. But it was the first time that anyone else said to me, 'No one else in the world is as stupid as you are.'" Kinoshita even said he felt sorry for Kawasaki's employees. Kawasaki endured Kinoshita's insolence. Kawasaki is short-tempered, but with fears of bankruptcy in his mind, he was willing to endure any embarrassment as long as he could get the assistance he needed.

Kawasaki was surprised by the conversation that ensued immediately after he showed Kinoshita a brochure of his company. Looking at the photos in the brochure, Kinoshita asked: "Why do you put things directly on the floor? Who devised this production line?" Kawasaki replied: "I did." "You are not stupid," said Kinoshita, "you're *very* stupid. What is the operating ratio of this robot?" "About 10 to 30 percent," said Kawasaki. "Did you borrow money to buy it?" "Yes." Kinoshita said: "You are hopeless."

Kinoshita continued to point out one problem after another. After the first meeting, Kawasaki was summoned to NPS's office every day. He would simply be told to come to the office at a particular time, regardless of his appointment schedule. One time Kawasaki did not have the time to sit through the entire meeting so he brought his younger brother, a company director, to the meeting. Kawasaki's plan was to leave the meeting early and have his brother handle the rest of it.

When Kawasaki arrived with his brother, Kinoshita told them both to leave. When Kawasaki asked why, Kinoshita replied that he would speak only to the president — the program would not succeed unless the president was fully committed to the program. Kawasaki's intention of using his brother as his substitute, Kinoshita said, showed that he was not fully committed. Kawasaki told his brother to leave and apologized for having brought him. He promised Kinoshita that he would come in person from then on.

NPS was demanding of Kawasaki. The president was summoned to NPS's office every day for two weeks as a test of his commitment. For two weeks, he listened to Kinoshita point out how incapable he was as a president and was asked whether he realized the suffering he would cause the employees if the company went bankrupt.

After the two weeks, Kinoshita told Kawasaki to visit Yokogawa Electric's Oume plant. Kinoshita said: "At the Oume plant, the workers process steel plates, paint them, and attach instruments to them, just like you do. Visit the plant, and think about how mistaken Kawasaki Electric's production method is." Kawasaki went to visit the plant, accompanied by his own plant executives.

The manager of the Yokogawa Electric plant said:

I've never visited Kawasaki Electric's plant. But I bet you aren't able to stand at one end of the plant, look across the plant, and see the opposite wall. I also bet that the workers are running around the plant like chickens with their heads cut off. I bet that you do your work in bunches.

The plant manager was correct about conditions at Kawasaki Electric's plant. During the tour of the plant, Kazuhiro Kawai, managing director of Kawasaki Electric, shouted: "President, this is it. This is what we've been looking for!" Kawasaki immediately went to see Kinoshita and said: "We have just come back from a tour of Yokogawa Electric's plant. I don't know much about factories, but the executives responsible for our plants say that Yokogawa Electric's plant is the embodiment of what they have been looking for. We want to join NPS." Saying that, he bowed his head to Kinoshita.

Kinoshita said: "Before you saw Yokogawa's plant, I bet you thought that NPS was just a cock-and-bull story." Kawasaki answered honestly: "Yes, I thought it was a little exaggerated." Seeing Yokogawa's plant, however, left Kawasaki with not a shred of doubt about what NPS could do.

Orderliness and Organization

Several days after the meeting described above, Kinoshita said: "I'll be visiting your plant in Yamagata." Kawasaki asked: "What should we do in the meantime?" Kinoshita answered: "Orderliness and organization. Orderliness means discarding everything you don't need. Organization means knowing where things are so that you can get anything the moment you need it." Kawasaki flew back to the Yamagata plant and personally supervised a plantwide cleanup campaign. Unnecessary items — enough to fill eighteen 11-ton trucks — were discarded. Kawasaki then waited for Kinoshita and Kozo Makise, an NPS instructor, to arrive.

A common practice when touring a plant is to walk through the plant in the same direction in which the goods flow. Most consultants and bank-employed research analysts who had visited Kawasaki Electric's plant had toured the plant in that order: from sheet-metal working to painting to assembly and finally to shipping. Kinoshita did not follow the routine. He and Makise visited shipping first, and moved upstream to assembly, painting, and sheet-metal working. They were told that there were other processes, such as designing, but Kinoshita said that there was no need to see them. He asked all group managers and higher executives to gather. When managers had assembled, Makise told them:

> It has been a long time since I had the chance to tour such an interesting plant. You probably don't realize this, but as I walked through the plant, I got the impression that all of you are working to hasten your company's bankruptcy. With the way you are working, the quickest way to postpone bankruptcy for three days would be to not work for three days.

Looking back to those days, Kawasaki says: "I realized that our company's group managers and those above thought that even though the company was in the red, the president would sell some of his assets, bring in the necessary cash, and somehow salvage the company. I was shocked to learn that that's the way they felt."

Kinoshita then addressed the crowd: "Our instruction is to produce one item at a time with one setup, to produce items just-in-time with the later processes determining the production quantity of the former processes." The managers listening did not understand what he was talking about. They felt that Kinoshita's advice would simply increase costs.

Noboru Kawasaki was convinced that he should introduce the NPS practices. The strongest opposition to his plan came from his younger brothers, who weren't convinced and thought that Noboru, the oldest brother, had come up with another stupid idea. One day Kikuo Suzumura yelled at Yutaka Kawasaki, one of the brothers who was also vice-president: "Hey, you are the second in command. Are you here to obstruct the top man?"

Many workers, especially those in marketing and sales, remained skeptical of NPS. Noboru Kawasaki had a reputation for being fond of whatever was new. Some workers said: "The president has retained some ridiculous consultants. The president must have gone crazy," or "The company will get worse if we use the NPS method." It was almost impossible to win the trust of the workers.

Bending Over Backwards

After beginning to use the NPS methods, the company posted a year-end loss of ¥70 million ($318,000) in March 1982, a current loss of ¥615 million ($2.6 million) in March 1983, and a current loss of ¥1.26 billion ($5.4 million) in March 1984. As the losses grew, so did the workers' mistrust of Kawasaki, who asked them to believe in NPS. When it became clear that the company would post a major loss for the third successive period, many workers gave up hope for the company. Because there were many electronics and other industries in Yamagata, it was easy for workers with a technical background to find new employment. Many line workers and managers left the company.

As this happened, Suzumura, empathizing with Kawasaki, said:

> As you follow the NPS practice, many of your employees, many of your personal friends, will leave the company. Don't try to change their minds. You must clasp your hands, watch them leave the company, and say: "Thank you very much. This cuts the monthly cost by ¥200 or ¥300 thousand ($800-1,200)."

At one time, the company's outlook was so bleak that one of the plant directors told his wife: "I am unlucky. But since this is the company I have chosen, I am going to work for it until it goes bankrupt. Be prepared for that." But even though prospects were poor, they were not hopeless. As Kawasaki says: "I was lucky I learned about NPS."

When Kawasaki Electric posted a loss of ¥700 million ($2.8 million) and had problems raising operating capital, Kinoshita personally visited the Long-Term Credit Bank of Japan and told the bank officials: "Please help Kawasaki Electric. If we can overcome the current problem, we will revive the company." This convinced the bank. Such words coming from ordinary consultants would carry no weight, and other consultants would not even think of doing such a thing. Shortly after that, Kawasaki Electric began a remarkable comeback. It was as if a critically ill patient, hooked up to a respirator and expected to die in a day or two, suddenly got up and walked away from the bed on her own two feet.

Many workers could not believe the quick turnaround. They said: "How can a company with a loss of ¥1.26 billion ($5.4 million) show a profit for this period? First of all, with our new sales practice, the size of an average order is smaller than last year's. How can you make a profit? That's impossible." Many in sales did not believe the figures that showed a profit. Some workers even thought that the company had resorted to window dressing.

In fact, the business environment was difficult. Among manufacturers of construction-related electrical components, it was only the electrical switchboard industry that had not gone through an industry shakeout since World War II. In other spheres, the lighting fixture industry was dominated by Toshiba, Matsushita, Hitachi, and Mitsubishi, four companies that accounted for over 90 percent of the market share in Japan. In the elevator industry, the four largest companies held a combined market share of 90 percent. Three companies held a combined market share of 90 percent in the disaster-prevention equipment industry. The only exception was the electrical switchboard industry, where 448 companies were members of an industry association, and more than 3,000 manufacturers existed in Japan. The demand for the industry's products totalled some ¥400 billion ($1.6 billion).

Kawasaki Electric and two manufacturers in Nagoya were generally acknowledged as the leading specialized manufacturers of electrical switchboards. However, the three companies combined had less than a 10 percent market share. Given this background, the industry was poised for a shakeout. Kawasaki spoke forcefully to his workers: "It is possible. If our own employees handled the books, I could have arranged for window dressing. However, the books are kept by the Long-Term Credit Bank. Window dressing is not possible. The profits are for real. We have achieved a profit with your help." Figures 3, 4, and 5 show the success of Kawasaki Electric's productivity and cost-cutting programs since joining NPS.

By the spring of 1985, the mood at Kawasaki Electric was optimistic. One of the workers told Kawasaki: "Mr. President,

Fiscal year	Sales (millions of yen)	Ordinary profit (millions of yen)
1982	9,448	− 615
1983	9,001	− 1,261
1984	10,140	143
1985 (forecast)	11,000	500

Number of workers / Fiscal year	Clerical, sales, engineering			Production floor operations			Total		
	Male	Female	Sub-total	Male	Female	Sub-total	Male	Female	Sub-total
1982	284	100	384	156	27	183	440	127	567
1983	270	91	361	159	26	185	429	117	546
1984	225	72	297	119	11	130	344	83	427
1985	212	50	262	120	28	148	332	78	410

Figure 3. Overview of Kawasaki Electric

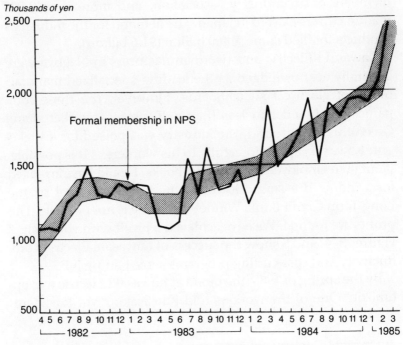

Thousands of yen

Figure 4. Kawasaki Electric Productivity Trend (monthly production in yen per employee)

I've been working here for more than ten years. During that time, not one good thing has happened. Why don't you do something to encourage us?" After hearing this, Kawasaki decided to visit the 1985 International Science and Technology Exposition held in Tsukuba, and invited all the employees to visit too. Kawasaki Electric had been a major supplier of parts used at the exposition. Kawasaki decided to tour the exposition, for business as well as for pleasure.

At the exposition, one worker looked at the group of employees together and said: "Look how many employees we have. We can do anything!" Kawasaki told the workers: "This visit has been very beneficial. If we all work hard together, we

Production items: Electrical switchboards, panel boards, control panels, relay panels, circuit breakers, various electronic equipment

Deployment		Plant	Sales
Point	1982	• Orderliness and organization in storage sites • Using assembly lines for panel-board assembly	
	1983	• Using lines throughout plant • Using kanban method for inventory control • Creating system for coordination of timing among different processess/Just-In-Time	• Creating proper consciousness among sales force (KCD seminars)
Line	1984	• Work improvement in manufacturing, using cycle time • Improving production floor to reduce number of processes • Standardizing • Achieving full participation • Using serial-number management/manufacturing one item at a time, using one setup in numerical order	• Creating system allowing employees to understand each role in overall flow of goods in plant (plant management from receipt of orders to recovery) • Stacking up improvements of shop floor and of actual goods Individual training and education of sales force
Plane	1985	Mobilizing sales and production people to standardize production	

Figure 5. Progress of the "Kawasaki Costs Down!" (KCD) Campaign

can revive the company. Let's believe in NPS." Kawasaki had a chance to hug and shake the hands of his employees and pledge to cooperate with them in improving the company.

It's Cheaper to Make It Yourself

Before receiving instructions from NPS, Kawasaki Electric plants were so full of equipment and work-in-process that it was virtually impossible to stand at one end of the plant and see the opposite wall. The workers were scurrying around the plant floor. They were always complaining that there weren't enough workers, equipment, or floor space.

However, once Kawasaki Electric adopted NPS's method of producing one item at a time, using one setup and a just-in-time production method, the amount of inventory and work-in-process continued to decrease. It was also possible to reduce the number of workers on a line by reducing the length of the line. This freed up labor to manufacture in-house what was previously subcontracted out.

Noboru Kawasaki did not initially believe the NPS instructors who said that in-house fabrication was cheaper than subcontracting out. The reason was that in the past Kawasaki Electric *had* fabricated all components in-house until Noboru Kawasaki and other second-generation managers convinced the late first president of Kawasaki Electric that it was cheaper and more efficient to contract out than to fabricate items themselves.

Suzumura used the following analogy to convince the skeptics:

Consider which is cheaper, subcontracting or in-house fabrication. Many think that contracting out is cheaper. But as an example, consider a family of five. If they ate out every meal and each meal cost ¥600 ($2.40) per person, the cost would be almost ¥10,000 ($40) per day. That would be almost ¥300,000 ($1,200) per month. However, if the parents cook at home for free, a well-balanced meal can be prepared for everybody for about ¥ 40,000-¥ 50,000 ($160-200) a month. This might be an extreme example of the benefit of in-house fabrication, but it is cheaper than contracting out.

Of course, NPS did not insist that everything be fabricated in-house. There were two exceptions to the rule. The first exception was that items Kawasaki Electric could not fabricate in-house for technical reasons could be subcontracted out; the other exception involved subcontractor relationships with companies founded by former employees of Kawasaki Electric who had had to leave Kawasaki Electric for reasons attributable to the company itself. Everything else had to be fabricated in-house.

NPS is frequently criticized for seeking to increase efficiency by increasing the work load on employees. For example, the NPS instructors noticed that there were too many chairs in Kawasaki Electric's plants. The instructors asked: "How many of you have wives who cook sitting down? They do it standing up. Working while standing up is the best. It is healthier than sitting down all day." The instructors requested that all chairs be removed from Kawasaki Electric's plants and that all work be performed standing up.

Workers believe it is more comfortable to work sitting down than standing up. When they were told to work standing up, their initial reaction was that NPS had increased the work load. However, it may be true that it is better to work standing up and be in charge of several jobs at once than to be sitting down all day at one place with a bent back. There is no doubt that workers initially feel tired after changing from a sitting posture to a standing posture. Some workers' legs may even swell up. However, the workers get used to standing up in a matter of days. Moving the body also prevents stiff shoulders and lower back pain.

This point becomes clearer when looked at from the other side. If, for example, a worker used to standing up and moving around at work is told to remain seated the whole day, that would be truly uncomfortable. Those used to sitting down feel that sitting down is the natural way of doing things. However, to those used to standing up, remaining seated is unnatural.

Doing It in Three Days instead of Sixty

NPS does not believe in labor intensification. According to its philosophy, labor intensification is tantamount to crime. Therefore, increasing the work efficiency does not mean more overtime. In fact, the amount of overtime at Kawasaki Electric has been reduced to one-third of what it was. Whereas it was once common for workers to work Saturdays and Sundays, it is almost unheard of now.

NPS does not require workers to huff and puff and sweat and work like machines. Rather, NPS tells management to "think of the workers' happiness." The NPS philosophy is:

> The company should not forget that it is using the precious time of the workers. The duty of management is to ensure that workers have free time to enjoy their lives. Workers have families. Young workers have boyfriends and girlfriends. The company must not waste the workers' precious time in overtime.

At any rate, NPS proved to be wonderfully effective in improving Kawasaki Electric. Noboru Kawasaki says: "I learned for the first time that working does not mean using a lot of workers. We now produce with less manpower and time. We now produce in three days or one week what used to take 60 days." Kawasaki himself is surprised at the turnaround.

Adoption of the NPS methods also resulted in more efficient use of space. Workers used to complain that the plants and offices were too small. Now, however, Kawasaki Electric has some 53,000 square feet of unused floor space. In May 1983, clerical offices that had been scattered over eight locations were consolidated and housed in one plant. This improved the harmony within the company. White-collar office workers tend to look down on blue-collar plant workers. However, when the office and production-floor workers were brought together, everyone realized they were all working for the same company. This is one of the intangible benefits of using NPS.

CHAPTER FIVE

The World Company:
Marketing What Is Fashionable Today

M ANY people believe sewing machines are best operated while sitting down. At the plant of World Company, a member of NPS, you won't see a sewing machine operator sitting down. Moreover, each worker handles not one sewing machine but several, moving from one sewing machine to another to oversee the operation of as many as four at a time.

NPS is concerned not with the efficiency of a single sewing machine but with the efficiency of the entire process. Overall efficiency is increased by having one worker oversee several machines and by leaving each machine running on its own while the worker checks the others. Of course, each machine is equipped with accessories that ensure that it runs in a straight line or along a predetermined curve to create the required sewing pattern. The machines also stop automatically if a thread is accidentally cut or the sewing pattern goes awry. There is no need for a worker to continuously monitor each machine.

The sewing machines monitored by one worker are not performing the same task. Each machine performs a different task: one sews sleeves, another collars, yet another, the fronts, and still another, the backs. By the time the worker makes a round of his or her machines, an article of clothing is almost sewn. This is the embodiment of NPS's philosophy of producing one item at a time.

In other garment factories, a worker operating a sewing machine usually watches a single machine, making sure a thread is not cut, the seam is straight, and so on. The traditional belief is that quality merchandise is produced only when one worker operates one sewing machine. Under the NPS philosophy, the worker's job ends when the fabric is placed on the sewing machine and the machine is switched on. Simply watching a sewing machine do its work is not considered real work. The machine is working, but the worker is not. NPS therefore tells the worker to do a different job once the machine is switched on and starts to operate. It is not possible to do another job while sitting in front of a sewing machine, so NPS requires the workers to remain standing.

Watching the speed at which the sewing machines operate at World's plant gives an insight into the NPS production method. At other garment manufacturing plants, sewing machines run at very high speeds. It is as if a sewing process is accomplished in mere seconds.

At World's plant, however, the sewing machines run slowly — so slowly that the needles move as if being driven manually. The pace is so slow it makes us think efficiency must be very low. One wonders if World's plant can produce enough to satisfy Japan's entire demand. I asked Hirotoshi Hatasaki, president of World, about this. He replied:

> It is not efficient to sew at very high speed. Each article of clothing must be sewn in sequence, from one process to another. If one sewing machine is very fast, you will have an increasing quantity of garments being sewn by that machine. Moreover, running a sewing machine at high speed means a greater number of defective items. Once a seam is sewn erroneously, it is impossible to do it over. It's better to sew at a slower pace with fewer defects.

Hatasaki's logic proves the futility of trying to increase productivity by sewing faster.

A Pilot Group Tries the NPS Way

When World introduced the NPS system and told its sewing machine operators that they would henceforth have to work standing up rather than sitting down, it met with strong opposition from the workers.

Some asked "Why?" Others accused World of overworking people and other abuses. But NPS instructors are willing to do things one step at a time. They do not impose the NPS philosophy all at once. They selected a small group of workers to try out the NPS way. The pilot group realized that working while standing up was healthier than sitting down all day and that being responsible for many jobs, not just one, made the work more enjoyable.

This is common sense. A worker seated the whole day in one place repeating the same thing over and over begins to feel like a robot. However, when the worker is allowed to become multi-talented, he or she develops a sense of joy or satisfaction in working. Moreover, since each worker operates several sewing machines at a time, productivity increases. Once the NPS method is accepted by a small pilot group, it spreads throughout the company like wildfire. World has enjoyed major successes since introducing the NPS method.

Sewing machines made to run with seated operators are too low to be run standing up. NPS did not tell World to replace their sewing machines with ones better suited for stand-up operation. One of the NPS beliefs is to not spend money on unnecessary capital investment. The seamstresses voluntarily took saws and hammers and fashioned legs and stands out of two-by-fours to raise the machines to a better height. At World's plant, one notices not only that the sewing machines and other equipment look handmade but also that they are laid out in a very efficient manner.

Winning by Manufacturing Only What Can Be Sold

Hirotoshi Hatasaki of World does not hide his joy at having joined NPS. He says:

> We are very lucky to have joined NPS because we're told that only one company can join NPS from any one industry. If we had heard about NPS at another time, it might have been too late. I think we were destined to join NPS. It has truly transformed the company.

The clothing industry is a difficult industry to survive in, constantly at the mercy of the whims of fashion. Numerous companies have enjoyed fleeting success. Against this background, credit must be given to Hatasaki's managerial skills and stability, as well as to his ability to predict fashion trends in order to sustain World's rapid growth and staying power as a leader of the fashion industry.

Hatasaki says: "Companies in our industry run into problems when the products they manufacture — and expect to sell — do not sell at all." Most bankruptcies occur in this industry because a company has too much inventory that just cannot be sold.

With the fashion industry, it is imperative not to manufacture what cannot be sold. Another way of saying the same thing is that it is important to produce efficiently only what can be sold. The ideal is to produce what can be sold, when it can be sold, and only in the amount that can be sold.

The fashion industry is competitive, with overall profits of each company varying widely. However, since the profit margin in merchandise pricing is about the same for every company, whether a company makes money is largely determined by the quantity of merchandise that remains unsold.

With the fashion industry, the bottom line is directly affected by the amount of waste that occurs. However, many clothing manufacturers insist on mass production. They cannot shed the business practice of selling large quantities on a small profit margin. The management of such companies is afraid that business will suffer irreparable damage once the practice of mass production and mass sales is abandoned.

The fashion industry has been sustained by the increasing affluence of the Japanese people. The companies now in the fashion industry have somehow survived in this difficult industry. However, it is also true that many clothing manufacturers are using the same old business practices even though society has undergone major changes. They predict a sales figure and mass-produce based on expected sales. They either enjoy a boom when the products sell well or go bust when they don't. The companies seem to lurch from one crisis to another. The days when such lax management could be tolerated are probably coming to an end. Hatasaki was looking for a modern production method to fit the new age. He heard about NPS, became convinced that it was his only ticket to survival, and decided to join.

It is impossible to convince your subcontractors when you yourself are not convinced. So, Hatasaki decided to first use the NPS method at three plants directly owned by World.

If a Car Can Be Produced in a Single Day . . .

Before World introduced the NPS method, it took about one month to produce a single jacket or a single dress. Everyone at World thought this was acceptable. When a request was made to speed up production time, the one month would be cut to 25 or even 20 days. That was considered quite an accomplishment.

However, when the production time for each jacket or dress, from beginning to completion, was precisely monitored, it was found that it actually took less than 1.5 hours. This meant that with the proper production method, it would be possible to produce each garment very quickly. World, like most other garment makers, produced clothing in batches of several thousands. Sleeves would be sewn, then collars, then pockets, and so on. This meant that it took a lot of time to finish even one garment because work was being done on so many at the same time. Those at World thought this was the proper production method and did not look for any other.

Hatasaki recalls: "It takes less than one day to produce a car. Why does it take days, even weeks, to produce a jacket or a dress? It makes you wonder."

Before NPS was introduced, work-in-process stacked up in many locations in the plants. NPS introduced at once a system to reduce inventory at each location. This eliminated the danger of overproducing products that would eventually go unsold. Eliminating excess production increased productivity and created a superb system that could better respond to customer needs. World introduced the NPS method at its three plants and is now aggressively promoting the method in ten affiliated plants.

In 1973, immediately after the oil crisis, World suffered from overproduction. Despite the popularity of World's products, it was impossible to sell jackets, dresses, and the like when housewives were desperately buying up toilet paper and detergents as an upshot of the oil crisis. Clothing was low on their priority list. World had been successfully riding the wave of high economic growth in Japan, using mass production based on planned output. It was impossible to stop the production lines, and the company had to suffer the consequences of an excessive inventory.

With planned mass production, semifinished goods are produced incessantly and it is almost impossible to stop production once it is started. Hatasaki realized that the production system had to be changed. He took command and managed to stop production. Until then, Hatasaki had believed that there was little profit in spring and summer clothes — that because World manufactures primarily knitwear, profits lay only in fall and winter clothing. Hatasaki realized that if overproduction continued, World would not make any profit. Hatasaki therefore made the production of spring and summer clothing more efficient. The result was that the spring and summer lines became profitable as well. World's products sold well the following year, making the company a good profit.

Even though World had improved the way its spring and summer clothes were produced, there was still a belief in mass production. Now that it has become acquainted with NPS, World's basic philosophy is to produce one article of clothing at a time. Whereas it used to believe that mass production reduced cost and improved productivity, the company has come to realize that mass production does not accord with present realities.

The production method used is critically important in the fashion industry. As Hatasaki says:

> We do not produce works of art. With art, value increases as time passes. With our products, what is one season old is no different from a used garment. You can't sell them even at half price. Men's clothing is not as sensitive to fashion. But with women's clothes, nobody buys them once they're out of style. The fashion industry is one of ups and downs.

Given this reality, NPS provides World with numerous advantages. For example, if it takes two hours to produce any garment, it is possible to wait until an order is received before producing and delivering. There is no need to carry an inventory or to predict what will be fashionable and then produce in advance, always a risky practice. Because production follows the receipt of an order, World does not need to discount to move its inventory, thereby strengthening its image as a brand.

In the apparel industry, where hordes of manufacturers have very unstable profit pictures, World has been remarkably successful: In 1984, its sales reached ¥130 billion ($563 million). When its subsidiaries are included, sales for the World group reached ¥190 billion ($823 million). Ordinary profit was ¥23 billion ($996 million). These figures stand head and shoulders above those of its competitors in the fashion industry. The ordinary profit for competitors Onward, Renown, and Wacoal was only a little over ¥10 billion ($43 million). Some observers feel that World is doing too well. World now owns a modern high-rise building in Kobe as well as several buildings at prime locations in the Kojimachi and Kudan districts of Tokyo. World was able to buy these buildings, most of which are used for office rentals, with its cash surplus.

Responding to the Specific Market

Hatasaki says: "It is true that it is faster and more efficient to produce sleeves, collars, and so forth, all at once and then sew the pieces together later. However, that production method becomes inefficient as lot sizes decrease. It is very difficult with large equipment meant for mass production to change the product line or to adopt high-diversity, small-lot production. High-diversity, small-lot production is the only way we can sell our products in this day and age. People's tastes are diversifying. Consumers are more individualistic. Some even say that each consumer comprises his or her own 'market.' We must produce a wide variety of products to satisfy the numerous markets.

"In the past, we produced in huge lot sizes, and our production level was much higher than that of our competitors. We were lucky to have sold what we produced. We didn't suffer from overproduction. If we were still using that production method, we might enjoy a few hit items, but we would also be saddled with goods that just wouldn't sell. In the end, we would see a loss.

"In the fashion industry, we must avoid overproduction. This is because overproduction usually leads to discounting. When you start discounting, your brand image suffers. A good brand image is most important.

"Take, for example, golfwear. Golfwear is of very high quality. But golfwear is overproduced and has to be discounted. Now everybody is wearing it, even the delivery boy from your neighborhood restaurant. It doesn't matter if the top golf professionals are also wearing it. Golfwear's image has suffered, and you won't be able to sell it at a high price anymore. People don't feel that they are wearing something exclusive.

"Feeling is important. It is important for a person to feel that he or she is wearing something well made. You wear a good necktie and you feel more confident. If your shirt is wrinkled, you don't feel like meeting people. In the fashion industry, feeling is very important. NPS's basic philosophy is to produce in lot sizes of one. If we can accomplish that, we can respond to any change. Of course, producing in lot sizes of one is not efficient. However, it allows you to respond to changes. You produce only as much as is actually sold. And, once you have the ability to produce in lot sizes of one, it is not difficult to produce in lot sizes of 20 or 30. If you are producing in a lot size of several thousand, as we used to, a minor design change causes a significant drop in production. Mass production is easy, but with mass production it is difficult to adapt to design changes.

"Moreover, mass production requires buying the raw fabric in massive quantities. Once you get the ball rolling, it's very hard to stop. You have to cut the fabric into numerous parts. If the product does not sell well, what are you going to do? The fabric has been ordered and cut into hundreds of parts. You have hundreds of finished sleeves. What can you do?

"But if you can stop production immediately it's a whole different story. For example, you have ordered the fabric, but the product isn't selling. If you have a system that can respond quickly to changes, you can stop production. You can change the design and use the fabric for other products.

"Take, for example, a restaurant. It serves many dishes: Japanese-style noodles, Chinese-style noodles, tempura, sushi, and so on. It would be stupid to cook ten days' worth of tempura because your hunch tells you tempura will sell well today. If the customers order noodles and sushi instead, the tempura will spoil. It is better to fry the tempura and cook the noodles after the customer orders them. Once you cook something, you can't go back to the raw ingredients. What are you going to do if you have tons of pork chops but the customers want noodles?

"In the fashion industry, we can adapt to design changes while still in the raw material stage, that is, when all we have are raw fabrics. Once you start sewing fabric into a garment, however, it's too late. NPS teaches us not to make that mistake."

Multi-Task Production: Abandoning Conventional Wisdom for Increased Adaptability

Hatasaki continues: "When you visit some factory and see component after component moving down a conveyor belt, you are impressed. But that is an illusion. It is better to have numerous small lines in a factory than a single large line. For example, think of your mother. She wakes up in the morning and turns on the rice cooker. Because cooking rice takes time, she does this first, even before washing her face. While the rice is cooking, she prepares the other dishes — eggs, salad, soup, and so forth. When everything's ready, she puts them on the table. You see, one person is doing many tasks.

"But modern factories are divided up into specialties. It's as if one person cooks the rice, a second person prepares the soup, a third person tosses the salad, a fourth person fries the eggs, and so on.

"At World, instead of restricting the workers to narrow specialties, we let them do many things concurrently. Instead of a linear product flow, envision a group of six or eight workers each working in a circle at several tasks. When each worker is assigned to one specialized task, one person may be idle while an adjacent worker is being rushed.

"That does not happen with 'multi-task production' [*nagara seisan* or 'production based on doing something while doing something else']. If there are 20 processes, there won't be 20 specialists. Instead there will probably be six or so workers each handling three or four processes. This means no more waiting. Goods will always be moving. There won't be piles of semifinished goods. Defective goods can also be checked by the workers. Each workday produces only finished goods. Work-in-process is eliminated.

"When you use assembly-line production and restrict workers to specialized tasks, they start believing that they can do only their specialized jobs. We are trying to develop multi-talented workers. What we are trying to do is not all that difficult. With proper training, a worker can learn more than one job. If you did only one thing over and over every day, the job would become boring. If, on the other hand, you are involved in every stage of production from start to finish, the job becomes more enjoyable and meaningful. Doing the same job every day is boring. A multi-talented worker knows that he or she is contributing. He or she begins to innovate.

"NPS also teaches us to avoid contracting out. Subcontracting involves a lot of supplementary work. You have to determine how much to order. There is transportation to consider, and writing out work orders. You aren't absolutely sure when the products will be delivered. You might have to pick up the products, again write an invoice, and inventory the delivery. It is a lot of work, and there's a lot of waste. It's usually much better to produce on your own. We tend to think that subcontracting cuts costs, but there are hidden costs and waste.

Using a subcontractor can be very inefficient, but many times we don't realize that.

"What is considered conventional wisdom is frequently nothing more than blind habit. Because it's been done that way, you never question it. It's blind faith. You can't develop something new unless you question the current practice and feel almost as if you have to change it.

"The mistaken belief that past success guarantees future success is to be feared most. We have been able to adapt to changes so far but that doesn't mean we can continue to do so. We were lucky to have adapted to changing times, to have succeeded. But we must not become complacent. Once you become complacent and start thinking you'll always be successful, you lose quickly.

"The important thing is to have a questioning attitude. The NPS methods went diametrically against conventional wisdom. In the past, I would watch my machines cutting yards and yards of fabric at once, and that made me feel good. You feel that you're really working. When I'd visit some other company's plant and see the latest equipment, I'd want to have that too.

"But now when I go to some plant and see the most modern equipment, I know that the plant is ponderous and not adaptive. You ask them to produce in a lot size of 10 or 20. They can't, and that's a very important point. The age of mass-producing the same thing at a low cost is over. The important thing now is to produce at the right time and in just the right amount.

"Of course, that's easier said than done. We were inexperienced. The instructors from NPS tell us that we are like kindergarten pupils. What the instructors are saying is that there is no end to improvement, that there are more things to be done. We now understand that there is no end to creative improvement and innovation. We don't have such audacious ambitions as to anticipate future fashion. All we are trying to do is create a company that can respond to the customer's desires."

CHAPTER SIX

Misawa Homes:
Soaring Productivity from
Small-Lot Production

MISAWA HOMES, a leader in the prefabricated-housing industry, joined NPS in September 1984. Chiyoji Misawa, president of Misawa Homes, first heard about NPS from Masayoshi Sakai, president of Ikuyo, a company with which Misawa Homes did business. Misawa says that he was not impressed with what he heard about NPS. What Sakai told him sounded like some junior high school nonsense. Misawa thought that Sakai was being taken advantage of by some cultlike, shady consultants.

Still, Misawa's company was facing difficulties. The housing industry was in a recession, and Misawa Homes was suffering from poor sales and low profit. Conventional wisdom held that success in the prefabricated-housing industry went to the company that reduced cost through mass production and mass sales. On the other hand, home buyers were no longer content with ready-made homes. They wanted their homes to reflect their own tastes.

Misawa Homes recognized these market trends and adopted a strategy to diversify their products. However, Misawa Homes' line of light-weight ceramic block homes, which they pushed aggressively, did not sell as well as expected. As far as wooden homes were concerned, the greater diversity of design sacrificed the advantages of mass production and mass sales. The upshot was a rapid increase in Misawa Homes' inventory of unsold houses.

Saddled with this problem, Chiyoji Misawa declared "an end to the land myth" and sold at a loss some of the land that had been purchased for a future housing development. He also announced major changes within the company, declaring that the former president was dead and that the new president would use new management techniques.

However, since announcing the results for the fiscal year ending March 1985, Chiyoji Misawa has been very cheerful. NPS's efficiency-increasing methods enhanced productivity significantly. Misawa is very bullish:

> We are certain that we shall show a major increase in profit for the year ending March 1986 [ordinary profit for the previous year had been ¥5.2 billion ($20 million)]. We will be celebrating the twentieth anniversary of the founding of our company in March 1988. Our goal is by then to increase ordinary profit to at least ¥20 billion ($80 million), and ¥25 billion ($100 million) cannot be ruled out.

Diverse Home Styles for Diverse Life Styles

According to Chiyoji Misawa, a person's life cycle is important for the housing industry. The Japanese used to spend their entire lives in one house. This, Misawa says, is changing and people are moving from one house to another as their economic situations change.

Americans reportedly move an average of eight times during their lives. Misawa say that the average Japanese couple passes through seven life stages; in each of these they may change homes for various reasons. The first stage is the twenties, when recent college graduates move into apartments. Misawa refers to this as "the rental-unit stage."

The next stage is the thirties. Young couples still find it difficult to afford a single-family home with land. They realize that renting does not increase their net worth. So they buy condominiums and thus begins the "condominium stage."

As their children are born and grow, their concern shifts to the children's education, health, and so forth. By now in their forties, the couples want a single-family home with a yard. This is a housing decision based on child-rearing. In the past, Misawa Homes aggressively employed a strategy of using "child-rearing" as a sales theme.

When couples reach their fifties, their position in society is secure and they have more leisure time. This starts a new stage in which the desire shifts to a more expensive single home. The decision here is based not on child-rearing but on enjoying their leisure.

When the couples reach their sixties, now retired, a possible choice is a three-story house, with the first story used for a small store or the like for a business based on a hobby, and the second and third stories used for living quarters. The couple spends their retirement days in this house, which serves as a home and also provides a source of income. Misawa Homes has a product line named "Domain" to fill this need.

The housing type for the aged is called the "condominium with care." This type is used by an invalid who needs daily assistance and medical care. Misawa Homes also identifies one other housing market, the "resort home," which is not linked to any particular age group.

From Standardization to Planning

Misawa Homes now features the seven life stages in its marketing strategy. Until recently, Misawa Homes had used the slogan, "A lifelong partnership through your home." The former marketing practice urged their customers to purchase and spend their entire lives in the same home and to enjoy the after-purchase service and maintenance provided by Misawa Homes. The company came to realize, however, that affluent home owners do not remain content with the same home; they move from one home to another, and the company had to build homes to accommodate this mobility.

This meant that Misawa Homes had to diversify into uncharted waters, namely, urban condominiums, condominiums with care, and resort homes. Although these new types of homes had been studied by the company's Environment Design Department for several years, they had never previously been built or marketed. It was now necessary to plunge into this new field.

In addition to the diversity based on life stages, another problem for housing manufacturers is diversity in house design. For Misawa Homes, a popular line of homes used to feature a semi-Western look; some called it the "Misawa look." Nowadays, the more classic, traditional European look is more popular. Designs such as "the modern look," reminiscent of the Museum of Modern Art in New York, "the casual look," and "the natural look" are also becoming popular. Among the more traditional Japanese designs, the *shoin, sukiya,* and *minka* styles are popular. These alone account for seven different designs now in use.

Thus, there can be 49 different combinations (7 × 7) of life stages and house designs. Moreover, the floor plan and quality of interior fittings can vary from home to home, creating even greater diversity. Furthermore, while a house may have a traditional Japanese exterior, each room in the house may be of a different style. The eldest son may want a room with a natural look, the eldest daughter a modern look, the second daughter a casual look. The interior finish can vary from room to room. Given this degree of demanded diversification, the builder has no choice but to resort to highly diversified small-volume production.

Until about ten years ago, Misawa Homes pushed standardized products. With the right decision, it was possible to sell three or four thousand homes of the same type. This is no longer true. A change has taken place from standardized to customized types. Even with prefabricated homes, there has to be diversity.

Chiyoji Misawa realized that he had to do something, that the old business practice was no longer viable. He had to increase the diversity of home types by tenfold or even a hundredfold without running up his inventory.

The diversification of home types had to be accomplished without increasing costs. Customers want all their wishes to be met but still want the cost to be low. This meant that high-diversity, small-lot production had to reduce costs as well.

Chiyoji Misawa, a man of action, decided to take a look at some of the plants using the NPS method. He visited Kawasaki Electric's Yamagata plant and Ihara Koatsu Tsugite's Akita plant. He did not at first understand what the NPS method was. But he did not give up. He visited other plants using the NPS method. Misawa says that he began vaguely to understand what NPS was trying to do after visiting about ten plants.

Misawa told Noboru Kawasaki, president of Kawasaki Electric, that he expected to see machines being used at Kawasaki Electric's plants to rationalize production. Misawa was surprised to see that Kawasaki Electric had removed many machines and human workers accounted for the rationalization.

Nevertheless, Misawa was not fully convinced. He was not sure that what worked with some other company would work well with his. Around the spring of 1984, after a lot of consideration, Misawa finally began to feel confident that NPS would be good for his company.

World Company Employees Convince
the Misawa Workers

With Misawa himself not fully committed in the beginning, it is easy to imagine that almost no employee at Misawa Homes fully believed in NPS methods.

When Noboru Kawasaki and NPS instructors visited Misawa Homes' Matsumoto plant, they were greeted by Misawa, the company's executives, and the production managers. After a plant tour, Misawa asked the NPS instructors to say whatever they felt about what they saw. One of the instructors, known for speaking his mind, said that the company was abnormal and that what he saw was not inventory but dead parts. Further attempts at automation, he said, would only serve to make the company worse — the production method was totally mistaken. The Misawa Home executive who had implemented the automation line responded that the NPS man was exaggerating and that he had no basis for saying such a thing.

When Misawa said that he was going to implement the NPS methods, all the workers at the plant objected. It was a natural reaction, knowing that NPS was going to undo what they had created over the last 20 years.

However, not long afterwards, an incident occurred that made believers out of the production-floor workers at Misawa Homes. Located next to Misawa Homes' Matsumoto plant is a World plant. Most of the workers at the World plant are women in their mid-twenties, who impressed Misawa Homes' employees by working late night after night. One day these workers made a tour of the Misawa Homes plant and pointed out all the problems with the company's production lines. The male workers at Misawa Homes, most of them close to retirement with almost 20 years of experience, had been shown up by these young female workers. After that, Misawa Homes' employees gave up their opposition to NPS and ceased their wrangling about the value of the NPS method.

World is a clothing manufacturer, and its employees have no interest in the production of prefabricated homes. However, after only one look at Misawa's plant they were able to point out the problems with the flow of goods and how the equipment was run. This is just one indication of the amazing abilities imparted by the NPS methods. Misawa Homes' employees had to take their hats off to NPS when they saw that workers well-versed in these methods could point out possible improvements in a production facility of an entirely different industry.

Many changes were made in Misawa Homes' Matsumoto plant after the introduction of the NPS methods. As in so many other manufacturing establishments, large-scale automation equipment had been installed in the Matsumoto plant during Japan's period of high economic growth. The practice was to mass-produce the products and ship them out as orders came in. In other words, until just recently, the plant was filled with much equipment, raw materials, work-in-process, and finished products.

However, visitors who now come to the Matsumoto plant are surprised. They say that the plant looks as if it were about to go bankrupt and that it has yet to undergo mechanization and labor reduction. They cannot believe that the plant belongs to Misawa Homes, the largest manufacturer of prefabricated housing.

In fact, many of the processes that would seem to benefit from mechanization are performed manually. Moreover, there are vast expanses of unused and unlit floor spaces in the plant. The plant does look as though it were in the midst of a production cutback.

Of course, production is not being cut back at the Matsumoto plant. The Matsumoto plant is where Misawa Homes started, and it is the most important of Misawa Homes' 27 plants, used as the main facility for producing large panels.

After joining the NPS Research Association, Misawa Homes has been using a production method based on NPS teachings, known as "MPS" (Misawa Product System). The preponderance of manual labor and the vast unused spaces on the factory floor are all the results of the use of MPS.

Chiyoji Misawa says: "We used to produce the panels in lot sizes of several dozens or several hundreds at the Matsumoto plant. Now, we produce in lot sizes of five. In a few months, we'll reduce that to a lot size of one." This is how far the Matsumoto plant has come.

The Matsumoto plant used to produce six different types of panel. Now that the plant has been transformed into a small-lot-size production plant, it produces more than 30 different types. That number will soon increase to more than 40. By eliminating the large equipment used for mass production and by bringing about a more responsive production system, lead time (the time it takes for raw materials to be turned into a finished product) has been reduced from two months to one day. The inventory, amounting to ¥2.3 billion ($96 million), was reduced to ¥1.1 billion ($47 million) as of July 1985 and has been brought down further to ¥700 million ($2.8 million).

Because NPS methods do not require the use of large equipment, capital investment, which was never less than ¥1 billion ($4 million) per year, has been reduced to about ¥300 million ($1.2 million) per year.

Houses Do Not Have Engines

The Nagoya plant had also been operating at a loss. Some in the company suggested the plant be closed. However, after NPS methods were introduced, productivity at the Nagoya plant soared, and the plant has been showing a profit since Spring 1985.

Kikuo Suzumura says:

When you hear "ceramic housing," it sounds impressive. But it is essentially a box with brick-like walls that are not especially complicated. First of all, there's no such thing as a "prefabricated home that moves." When you think about it, cars and houses are similar. They're each basically a box. Cars have extra parts such as an engine and four tires. As far as the number of parts is concerned, a car has more parts than a house.

So Misawa Homes' Nagoya plant manufactures simple homes yet operates at a big loss. You wonder what they are doing. What it boils down to is that they invested a lot of money in equipment for producing things that were more popular than expected. Once the equipment was installed, they had to produce in order to keep the equipment running. They felt that they had to have many different molds for pouring the blocks. They have so many molds that they fill the entire plant. This problem could easily have been solved by making molds that can be formed into different shapes. However, they insisted on creating a different mold for each shape, a very wasteful practice. This is typical of plants that operate in the red.

At any rate, Misawa Homes used to manufacture about 20 different types of components every day. They are now trying to increase that by tenfold, to about 200 different types. Moreover, the inventory is to be reduced to one-tenth. Misawa also says that productivity at the Matsumoto and Nagoya plants will be doubled and tripled, respectively.

Misawa says doubling productivity is not all that difficult. The company needs only a system that allows the same workers to do their job in half the amount of time and to use the time saved for some other job. The other job can be the in-house fabrication of what was previously subcontracted out. This will further reduce cost.

Chiyoji Misawa says he realized after introducing the NPS method that he was a total amateur in management and that Misawa Homes had done relatively well in the past only by riding the wave of Japan's high economic growth. The first thing that surprised Misawa after introducing NPS methods was the realization of how poorly his plants had been run. He admits:

We thought that our plants were operating at 100 percent. We realized, however, that they were actually operating at only about 25 percent. Even when it was so busy that workers had to work overtime, the equipment was working at 25 percent. However, everyone thought that an operating rate of 25 percent was really efficient. We didn't realize that the equipment was idle 75 percent of the time. Hence, doubling the productivity entailed increasing the 25 percent to 50 percent. We can still double even that figure. However, realizing that an operating rate is too low is difficult. Common sense says that it is impossible for a plant to operate 10 or 15 years with its equipment working only 25 percent of the time. But it is possible.

To simplify what happens at Misawa Homes' plants, raw lumber is placed on a piece of equipment. This constitutes work. The equipment is automated and workers watch the lumber being moved by the machine. It sounds good to say that the worker is "monitoring" the operation to prevent defects.

However, the worker is not really working while the machine is running on its own. In other words, real work is done for only a few seconds when the lumber is being placed on the equipment. NPS refers to the act of watching the lumber move along the machine as *loafing*. It is better to position the equipment so that one person can monitor two or three machines.

Misawa uses the following analogy to explain this:

When you go to a golf course, the swinging of the club to hit the ball probably lasts for about one second. So if you swing the club 100 times, the work takes 100 seconds. But when you go to a golf course, you spend two or three hours there for that 100 seconds. The walking and the practice swing you take before actually hitting the ball are not in themselves golf. Golf is the hitting of the ball. This means that in golf, one spends three hours to do a job that takes only 100 seconds. This is true of working too. The true working time is usually minimal compared to the time spent doing secondary things like just walking around.

Work, Too, Can Make Waste

Misawa adds:

People think it's strange when I say this, but it's true. Look at your own datebook. I have appointments with 11 people today. I'm supposed to be working hard this very minute. But because I spent time in idle gossip, the amount of time spent in real work is very small. Sometimes all you want to do is spend three or five minutes with someone to say "How are you?" or something like that, but you end up spending a half hour or an hour. I'm sure this is true of everybody.

Office workers come to work in the morning and supposedly spend eight hours working at the office. But I bet you that their real working time is probably not much more than two hours. So what we are doing at our company is not that surprising. It's just a confirmation that there's too much waste. Even Toyota says that the time spent in real work is only about one-tenth of the total time put in. That sounds about right.

It is not easy to recognize waste as waste. In building a home, careless design errors occur. Workers may spend two or three days looking for a door knob or preparing documents for a door knob that costs ¥3,000 ($12). The total labor cost may reach ¥100,000 ($400). Whether or not the door knob can be found immediately depends on how well information is organized. This is one reason why NPS always stresses orderliness and organization first.

One other event shocked Misawa. When Misawa Homes estimated the cost of exporting a plant to Korea, the projected investment came out to be ¥5 billion ($20 million). When this estimate was shown to an NPS instructor, he came back two hours later with improvements and an estimate of ¥2 billion ($8 million). When the instructor's suggestions were followed, the project only cost ¥1.8 billion ($7 million). These experiences truly taught Misawa to appreciate the difference between those who know and those who don't.

This difference can be significant. Computer manufacturers and equipment manufacturers, for example, always tout the convenience of their products, claiming that using them will increase productivity. This is natural. They have to sell their products. Of course, when you only look at the time the equipment is running, it is truly efficient. If the equipment is idle seven hours out of eight, however, the user's efficiency can improve by one-eighth at the most. Although the equipment may not be running most of the time, you remember the time that it is running and you get the impression that it is very efficient. Moreover, even if the machine produces quickly, if what is produced cannot be sold, it is the same as if the machine were not running.

The wise user with the proper production know-how will recognize these shortcomings and find better ways of doing things, selecting the best method for the plant. Users without the technical skill or know-how, however, tend to blindly follow what the equipment manufacturer or the computer vendor suggests. This becomes costly. It is important to realize that cost-cutting is difficult without production skill or know-how.

For example, the need to subcontract arises when management expects workers to produce what they are not capable of producing. Management then thinks subcontracting will be cheaper. Although it may be cheaper to manufacture a piece of equipment in-house, they end up buying expensive, less efficient equipment from an outside source. Worse, the division of labor inside the company ends up spreading the waste.

Since joining NPS, Misawa Homes has been creating a competitive corporate structure capable of cost reduction. The estimated production cost for 1984 for Misawa Homes' prefabricated products was 68 percent. The company is confident that this figure can be reduced to 60 percent during 1985 and to 55 percent during 1986. Misawa Homes is learning how to enter the ranks of big business.

————

CHAPTER SEVEN

Yokogawa Hokushin Electric:
The Dyer Who Wears White

W HEN Shozo Yokogawa, president of Yokogawa Electric (now known as Yokogawa Hokushin Electric) — who is credited with guiding Yokogawa Hewlett-Packard into a highly profitable business — met Mikiya Kinoshita, then president of Ushio Inc., Yokogawa was surprised to be asked: "Do you work in a warehouse at this plant?" Kinoshita then rudely told him: "This company will surely go bankrupt."

Until the oil crisis in 1973, Yokogawa Electric's business had grown well, supported by a general trend among industries to modernize and increase their capacity. However, demand slumped following the oil crisis, and the number of competitors increased. It was a dogfight for survival among Yokogawa Electric, Hokushin Electric, Toshiba, Hitachi, and others. Cost competition was naturally severe. Some said: "Nippon Steel and the other iron and steel companies are good not only at pounding iron but also at pounding down the price."

One condition working in Yokogawa Electric's favor was the difficulty faced by foreign manufacturers in entering the Japanese industrial instrument market — even though it was not a protected industry. The Japanese users knew that industrial instruments had to be produced essentially one at a time, and that time-consuming maintenance requirements made it unattractive for foreign manufacturers to enter the market.

However, competition among domestic manufacturers kept intensifying. It was imperative for manufacturers to reduce their costs. Moreover, industrial instruments have traditionally come in very diverse product lines. Shozo Yokogawa said: "We are like concubines. If we don't keep our patrons happy, we'll be cast aside. We have to produce a different product for each customer, and at a low cost."

It was in 1980, after suffering successive years of reduced profits, that Yokogawa established "halving costs" as a goal. Michio Katagiri, managing director of Yokogawa Electric, had been studying Toyota's kanban method as a cost-cutting tool. One day while Katagiri was thinking about ways of halving the company's costs, he thought about Mikiya Kinoshita of Ushio Inc., whom he had met earlier.

Katagiri visited Ushio Inc.'s Kobe plant. At that time, Ushio Inc. was pursuing the policy of producing one item at a time. Katagiri saw what Ushio was doing and realized that this was the way to go. At a meeting of the Yokogawa Electric directors, Katagiri presented his idea for halving costs. As soon as he had he finished his report, he encountered fierce opposition. Many said that there was no way that Katagiri, who had come up through sales and marketing, would understand production and that his proposal would never cut costs.

However, after listening to Katagiri, Shozo Yokogawa said: "What Katagiri is saying is very different from what anyone has suggested in the past. It's just different enough. Let's give it a try." In November 1980, Katagiri began work on creating a model production line.

As Empty as a Dance Hall

After the NPS Research Association was founded in January 1981, Yokogawa heard about it and repeatedly visited

Kinoshita, who had become the NPS director, requesting that Yokogawa Electric be admitted to membership. However, Kinoshita declined each time, saying: "If a big company like yours joined NPS, it would be like placing a shark in a fishbowl. You'll just upset the other companies."

Kinoshita, however, eventually agreed to visit one of Yokogawa's plants. The visit was on April 1, 1981 — April Fool's Day. Katagiri, ever impatient, had already begun running the model line in his own way. Kinoshita and the NPS instructors who saw the model line levied one criticism after another and left some homework for Katagiri.

Katagiri wanted at least to finish the homework. He sought help from others and, with the help of a number of workers, removed all the conveyor belts. There were, as one would expect, many conveyor belts. He finally created a semblance of a system capable of producing one item at a time.

Somehow Katagiri managed to find 700 square meters (7,532 square feet) of unused factory floor space from the 1,500 square meters (16,140 square feet) that were formerly used. When the NPS instructors came back to Yokogawa Electric several days later, they were surprised with what they saw and congratulated Katagiri.

At that time the prevailing opinion was that there was not enough floor space and that a new building had to be built. Lack of warehouse space seemed so pressing that approval had already been given for starting the construction of a ¥500 million ($2.5 million) warehouse in May, 1981. Building permits had been received from the municipal office of Musashino City. Plans were drawn up and contracts signed. However, the removal of conveyor belts in April created so much unused space that the warehouse construction was placed on hold.

The plant was radically modified over the next six months. So much unused floor space was created that the plant resembled a dance hall. Some said that it was so vacant you could almost catch a cold just standing in it. It was then that the workers and management realized what Kinoshita meant when he asked: "Do you work in a warehouse at this plant?" Some on the production floors had complained about the NPS methods, but even they eventually acquiesced in the new method.

Using Idle Resources to Reduce Costs

NPS's policy is to not buy, build, or use something new. Before it joined NPS, Yokogawa Electric's annual capital investment had been about ¥5 billion ($20 million). After introducing NPS methods, that amount was cut in half.

How capital investment can be cut in half while maintaining a profitable business is explained as follows: Producing one item at a time reduces inventory. A reduced inventory means no more overproduction. No overproduction means installing less equipment. Installing less equipment means less capital investment.

In other words, too much inventory means overproduction. Once you start producing only what you need, people and machines become idle. The idle resources can then be used for in-house fabrication, eliminating subcontracting.

If you don't buy new equipment, hire new people, build new buildings, or subcontract out, costs naturally come down, and profits go up. This is the basic mechanism of NPS.

Another important mechanism is the following:

Reduced inventory → reduced debts → reduced burden of
interest payments.

If a subcontractor delivers products in large lots, he or she receives correspondingly large payments. This is business. The party hiring the subcontractor, however, tends to order too much. To avoid the inconvenience of having to pay multiple invoices, the manufacturer orders 100 or even 1,000 units instead of 50. The delivered goods are stored in a warehouse, which generates storage costs.

Subcontracted goods can often be made in-house on under-utilized equipment. When you start producing one item at a time, you can readily observe when a machine is idle and that it is not being used. If someone suggests buying a new machine, the manager can say: "That machine is not being used. Use that machine." The manager may hear many reasons why the existing machine cannot be used. However, most reasons have something to do with setup. The manager can then say: "Alter the machine so that it is not so hard to set up." This usually puts an end to a request for a new machine.

Technicians and engineers want to produce as much as possible once a setup is in place. This creates waste and an excessive amount of work-in-process. Having the flexibility to produce one item at a time prevents overproduction. This reduces waste.

The First Junior High School Student

Suzumura is frequently seen these days talking joyfully: "NPS has its first junior high school student. What I mean is that Yokogawa's Kofu plant represents our ideal. The NPS member companies that are still like kindergarten or grade school students should visit and study the Kofu plant and implement the right things at their own plants."

Each automatic flow-rate recorder produced on the main line at the Kofu plant has a different set of specifications — each has a different shape and purpose. In other words, the Kofu plant produces goods strictly one at a time. Production of a recorder starts in the plant two hours after the order is received by the sales department. Parts fed from sub-lines are assembled without error on the main line to produce one finished product after another.

The delivery time has been greatly reduced. The lead time (the time from receiving an order to shipping the finished item) has been reduced from one month to two days in some cases. It should become possible in the near future to ship tomorrow what is ordered today, yet the company's cost is no higher than that of other manufacturers. All these things make Yokogawa more competitive, and, in fact, Yokogawa Kofu has no serious competition for its products.

An interesting fact is that Yokogawa Hokushin manufactures and sells automation equipment to other companies. Yokogawa therefore helps other companies achieve "labor-less operation." However, Yokogawa does not use labor-saving equipment or pursue factory automation at its own plant. On the contrary, the emphasis at the model Yokogawa Kofu plant is on fully using the talents of its workers.

When Yokogawa's sales and marketing departments insisted that the production departments utilize laborless operation so that the Kofu plant would be a showcase for customers, Shozo Yokogawa said no:

> We should remain the dyer who wears white but gets rich by coloring cloth for others. There are two types of factories in the world — those that benefit by following the policy adopted at our plant and those that benefit by automation, by using what we sell. It is not true at all that to sell factory automation, your plant must itself be a model of factory automation.
>
> Think well. If the dyer wore clothes dyed a particular color, customers might complain if the color didn't suit them. If the dyer had to dye his clothes a different color each time he visited a different customer, he'd go broke. So, he dyes his clothes white so that he can visit any customer without receiving a complaint. White is well suited to the dyer.

Yokogawa Electric merged with Hokushin Denki in April 1983. Yokogawa Hokushin Electric is now a top manufacturer of instruments not only in Japan but throughout the world. It should be noted that Yokogawa Electric was able to merge with Hokushin Electric because of the strong business foundation Yokogawa had established, thanks to its adoption of NPS methods. If Yokogawa Electric had not implemented NPS production methods, the merger with Hokushin Electric probably could not have taken place and, even if it had, would probably have resulted in the bankruptcy of the new enterprise.

It is true that the merger with Hokushin temporarily slowed Yokogawa Electric's growth. However, NPS is quickly being introduced in former Hokushin plants. Once the rationalization and streamlining of former Hokushin Electric operations is completed, Yokogawa Hokushin is expected to grow even faster as one of the most profitable companies in the industry.

CHAPTER EIGHT

The Skylark Restaurant Chain: Defrosting the Refrigerator

*T*HE Skylark restaurant chain grew rapidly during the last ten years, maybe too quickly. The rapid growth revealed organizational and management shortcomings.

Tasuku Chino, president of Skylark, first heard of NPS in the summer of 1981, making Chino one of the first to know about the association. At that time, Chino had decided to list his company on the stock exchange and was searching for a new corporate philosophy and system that would allow renewed growth of the company. Chino met Kinoshita and came away convinced that NPS's philosophy would benefit Skylark. Chino says he felt predestined to come in contact with NPS.

In the beginning, Chino could not fully understand how the NPS philosophy, based on the kanban method, could be adapted to a restaurant chain like Skylark. Chino thought that kanban was a production method that applied only to manufacturing.

However, closer observation showed that the restaurant business was nothing more than production based on orders. A customer comes to a restaurant, orders what he or she wants, eats it, and leaves. The restaurant produces what the customer wants. For a restaurant to prosper, it must serve good food quickly — so that the customer is not kept waiting — and at a low price. However, many restaurants do exactly the opposite.

Even though the restaurant industry seems to have gone through a period of modernization and rationalization, the industry still tolerates a lot of waste. For example, Skylark owned a large refrigeration facility at an industrial park in Higashimatsuyama, Saitama, which proved very wasteful. There is an enormous difference in taste between food cooked with fresh ingredients and food cooked with ingredients that are first frozen and then thawed out. The ideal would be to receive an order from a customer and prepare the food on the spot. The large refrigeration facility was used for preserving foods cooked in advance based on expected sales. But a large storage facility is unnecessary if a system is developed for delivering foods to restaurants only when needed.

From Industrial to Home-Size Pots

The worst example of the problems caused by mass production at Skylark was the soups. Bathtub-size vats were used to cook large quantities of soup at the Higashimatsuyama plant. However, customers are not satisfied with only one type of soup. They don't want just beef stew — they want onion soup, broth, consomme, and so on, so Skylark prepared large quantities of each variety. Preparing, packaging, and refrigerating these huge amounts of each soup cost the company immensely for refrigeration space, electricity, and storage. Money was spent like water, and the capital turnover was fearfully low.

NPS told Chino to stop these cooking and delivery practices. It instructed him to prepare soups in lots of 30 or 40 servings instead of 400 or 500. This meant using only the bottom part of the huge vats.

The employees complained: "Cooking so little in such a big pot is wasteful. Why don't we cook all at once?" The NPS instructors said: "You say it is wasteful. Do you want to be more wasteful and overproduce? That will only result in your salaries being cut." If the workers can understand that, they won't mind using smaller pots, preparation time will be reduced, and the fuel bill will be lowered. Less expensive pots and pans used in ordinary homes can be used. If it becomes necessary to cook more, all that is needed is to repeat the cooking procedure.

The Higashimatsuyama plant was originally designed to meet the needs of only 300 of Skylark's restaurants. As of the end of 1984, the plant was serving all 420 Skylark restaurants. By then, almost all of the mass-production equipment had been removed from the plant. Simple equipment and a single-item production method were put to use. With an improved distribution system in place, the huge refrigeration facility was emptied, yielding enormous cost savings. This is a good example of the difference that a production method can make.

With the super-rationalization efforts based on NPS methods, Skylark's management became confident that the restaurant chain could keep profits increasing at a rate of 15 to 20 percent per year. There is no doubt that Skylark became the strongest of the many restaurant chains.

Increasing Customer Flow through Faster Service

Skylark is improving not only its production practices but its distribution method as well. The Higashimatsuyama plant is located strategically close to the Kanto and the Tohoku districts but is rather far from the Kansai district. Skylark once had plans to build a new plant in Kansai, but the vastly improved production at the Higashimatsuyama plant, coupled with a more responsive distribution system, has solved the distance problem.

According to Chino:

The number of restaurants has increased by 40 percent since we joined NPS. If we were operating in the old way, we would have needed 50 percent more warehouses and plants by now. We haven't done that at all — and we have space to spare. For example, our automatic refrigeration facility became empty three months after we joined NPS and our overall inventory has been cut in half. We have a potential plant site in the Kansai district. Without NPS, we would have had to start building a new plant there. Now, however, we have no plans to do so.

Customer service has also changed greatly since Skylark introduced the NPS methods. Customers feel that a waitress or waiter is there and ready when they want to order. It was not this way in the past. There is a simple explanation. The overall operation of the restaurants was reevaluated in the light of NPS and kanban methods to see how customer requests could be met with the fewest possible workers. It was found that just having an attitude of satisfying the customers' needs increased the time spent on the dining room floor by 30 percent.

The kanban method is used not just in production, but also for keeping the restaurants clean. All of the tasks that need to be done in the restaurant are written on kanbans [signboards or cards]. Different color codes are used to differentiate those things that must be done daily, weekly, and so on. How the task is to be done is written on the other side of the kanban. If a manager is replaced or takes a vacation, everyone else knows what to do by reading the Kanban. The system ensures it.

The kanban approach and NPS methods have led to the best way of keeping a restaurant clean.

The restaurant industry in general, not just Skylark, is known for numerous wasteful practices. Loss of time and opportunity and food spoilage are just a few examples. If a customer is served quickly, he or she will leave quickly. This does not mean kicking the customer out. It just means that the customer turnover rate increases when customers are served quickly, and decreases when customers are served slowly.

Slow service means the restaurant's seating capacity is wasted. For example, four diners come to a restaurant and order curry and rice, hamburgers, steak, and noodles. Suppose the restaurant decides it is better to cook several servings of the same order rather than to prepare one serving at a time. So the restaurant waits until five servings of curry and rice, hamburgers, steak, or noodles are ordered before preparing them. The diners will have to wait a long time before their meal is served. They will probably get angry and never come back.

Preparing goods in lots inevitably creates such inconveniences. If goods are produced one at a time, it is possible to create different things at the same time and to serve all diners in the same party at the same time. This means the party will come and leave in a shorter time. Some people fear that increasing the restaurant's seating turnover lowers the quality of service, which, in turn, drives customers away. Actually, the reverse is true.

From Mass Production to Individual Attention

Chino adds:

Now that Japan is affluent, the consumption pattern is naturally becoming more individualized. It is very difficult to respond to a diversity of needs with a mass-production, mass-consumption approach. Providing the same thing to everyone is of course easier. But the company that grows is the company that can provide individual attention. Some may say that it is impossible to provide individual attention. They may be right. However, the companies that survive the stiff competition in the restaurant industry are those that believe that individual attention is possible and then render it.

In this age of abundance, the restaurant industry can grow simply by serving quality food at a low price while providing the joy of eating out. Lower prices allow people of lower income to eat in restaurants more often.

Skylark is gradually changing from a restaurant chain that forced its own requirements on the customers to one that provides individual attention based on customer needs. Customers naturally get tired of seeing the same menu all the time. Skylark is diversifying by opening a Japanese-style restaurant called Ashiya and a restaurant called Yesterday, with a more casual atmosphere. Skylark also started a fast-food fried chicken chain in the summer of 1985.

It is becoming increasingly difficult to meet the needs of all Skylark chain restaurants with a mass-production, centralized kitchen approach. Chino says:

The belief that mass production increases efficiency is an illusion. We made a mistake when we built a large plant and a warehouse. Whenever we have visitors, we show them the facility. They are impressed and say, "You can run a restaurant chain because you have such large facilities." But, in actuality, we regret having built such large facilities, and we do our cooking and preparation in a small facility that is hidden behind the large plant. The small facility looks like something you might find in China.

Customers will remain loyal to a restaurant as long as they are served fresh food quickly and at a reasonable price. Chino, a true believer in NPS production methods, says: "Going with NPS was our best decision."

CHAPTER NINE

The Kibun Food Company: Cutting Waste in a Perishable Food Operation

N OT MANY people under-
stand what Taiichi Ohno
means when he says: "Building automobiles and making
boiled-fish paste (*kamaboko*) are the same." To most people,
automobiles are assembled from tens of thousands of parts
using the most modern production methods while boiled-fish
paste is nothing more than ground fish that has been steamed
on a wooden plate.

When Mikiya Kinoshita was president of Ushio Inc., he invited Masahito Hoashi, president of Kibun, to visit his production plant, which was using Toyota-style production. Hoashi
declined for some time, saying that Kibun's production method
was different from methods used for producing automobiles.
However, Hoashi was surprised when he finally visited Ushio's
Himeji plant in the summer of 1979 with some of his friends.
By then a year had passed since the Toyota-style system had
been introduced at the Himeji plant.

There were two production lines at Ushio's plant: one line
based on the old production method and the other using
the new method. The old line looked impressive with equipment lined up in a neat row. The new line looked very ordinary. Hoashi noticed, however, that goods were flowing

along the new line without stopping. He was told that even though the new line looked unimpressive, its productivity was much higher.

Hoashi was captivated to learn that the new method had improved productivity. But what impressed him most were the words of one of the instructors, who said that the production method was based on a philosophy of treating the workers well. Food manufacturers must trust their workers. It would be very easy for a worker to tamper with a food production process — a scary thought. For this reason, the Kibun company had always promoted the well-being of its workers. The starting point of NPS's philosophy was to eliminate waste so that the workers could enjoy their lives to the fullest. The NPS instructors also said that it is disrespectful to force a worker to work on a job that adds no value.

An Open-Air Noodle Shop Is the Ideal

What Ohno means when he says that "cars and boiled-fish paste are no different" is that the only way for a company to survive in this age of high-diversity, small-lot production is to produce better goods faster and at a lower price than one's competitors. Moreover, Kibun's products, including the boiled-fish paste, are mostly perishable goods that must be produced quickly and shipped promptly to market. With cars, consumers do not care about their production date. With Kibun's products, the production date is displayed, and customers shun anything old. In this sense, it is more important for Kibun than for automobile manufacturers to produce goods quickly and ensure that all products are promptly sold.

Hoashi says:

The ideal food manufacturer is the open-air noodle shop. At such a shop, food is prepared after the customer places an order. They serve the food quickly and receive the payment. Any leftover ingredients are used the next day.

There is no inventory and no surplus. They have the know-how to produce only after an order is received. We have tried to incorporate the production method of an open-air noodle shop in our business.

Such a production process eliminates waste. Ideally, goods are produced after an order is received and then quickly delivered to the refrigerated section of a market. Actually, however, at many points in Kibun's production line products just sat. Kibun's distribution system was also inefficient, with the products first delivered to a central point then shipped to retail stores and supermarkets. Products are now delivered directly to the customers.

Kibun's plant has undergone significant changes since the introduction of NPS. When an NPS instructor saw raw ingredients while visiting the plant, he would ask the purpose of storing the ingredients. If final products were stacked at the end of a line, he asked if storing the products there improved them. If he saw products moving on a long conveyor belt, he would ask whether the taste improved as the product moved on the conveyor belt. If the answer was no, he would say: "The conveyor belt uses electricity and spoils the products. Stop using the conveyor belt." The instructor might ask: "How long does it take for a product stored in your warehouse to be shipped out?" If the answer was "around 12 hours," he would ask: "Does storing it for 12 hours improve its freshness? Is the warehousing free?"

The instructor might also ask: "How many days' worth of raw ingredients do you have in the plant? How much of the raw ingredients will you use today? Is there any advantage in storing the raw ingredients together?" If the answer was no, he would say: "Why don't you store only what is needed today?" These question and answer sessions eventually resulted in a reduced inventory and better use of funds. If surplus funds were created, the instructor would ask: "Will holding on to the surplus funds increase them?" If the answer was no, he would say: "Repay your loans." This cut down Kibun's indebtedness.

Beware of Regression

It is not true that introducing NPS produces only benefits. Hoashi also experienced difficulties. During the general meeting of the NPS Research Association in January 1985, Hoashi had to bow his head and weather a storm of criticism. He remembers: "People were saying that I, as president, was personally responsible for the company's poor performance and should resign. I had to listen to this in front of my company executives. I was so embarrassed."

Kibun had introduced the NPS method in 1980 and the following year posted the highest profit ever. What followed, however, was disastrous. Those who still believed in the old production method were not happy with the good results. Many employees looked for every little fault in the NPS methods. Conditions on the production floors had become chaotic during the last three years.

The top management at Kibun realized that they had erred in the way the NPS methods were introduced. At Kibun, the sales arm had traditionally been stronger than the production departments. Management tried once again to instill the NPS philosophy in the Kibun group of companies, this time supporting its production operations rather than overemphasizing sales. Finally, starting in 1984, Kibun's profits began to increase even though sales dropped. Production's inferiority complex is now gone, and they now see that the function of the sales department is to sell what the production people produce.

Kibun has over 20 plants throughout Japan. The plant managers hold voluntary study sessions, something unheard of before the introduction of NPS. The prevailing attitude was: "Your plant does it your way, but my plant will do it my way." Now the attitude is for all to learn from one another and cooperate for the continued growth of the company.

CHAPTER TEN

Asia Securities Printing: The Stockless Method as a Powerful Weapon

*A*SIA Securities Printing (or Asia Printing) celebrated its fifty-fifth anniversary in 1985. This company specializes in the printing of securities, a high-value-added production. The amount of printing done per job is small, however, and the amount of equipment and factory space used need not be great. This is one reason that Asia Printing can conduct all of its printing at a small facility in Toranomon, Tokyo.

There is no doubt that Asia Printing's high profitability (as compared to that of the other printing businesses) stems from handling securities, a high-value-added product. However, their implementation of the NPS method has allowed Asia Printing to achieve an even higher rate of profit.

There are many reasons. The first is that NPS convinced Asia Printing not to stock supplies of printing paper as it had done before. Presently, paper is ordered daily for the following day's printing requirements. If paper is needed in the afternoon, the supplier will deliver it in the afternoon. This system has eliminated the need for a paper warehouse. Because there is no inventory, money is not tied up in inventory, and interest on indebtedness is reduced. Labor is not wasted in running a warehouse.

Printing securities is a demanding task. Each security must be carefully printed with a serial number, the name of the stockholder, and so forth. For example, if one person owns one 10,000-share stock certificate and three 1,000-share stock certificates, his or her name is printed on the four stock certificates in a block. After one owner's certificates are printed, the presses are reset to print those belonging to another. The next person's portfolio may consist of five 1,000-share stock certificates and two 5,000-share stock certificates. The job is repetitive and labor-intensive.

One-third of Asia Printing's sales is derived from the printing of securities, one-third from printing financial reports, notices of stockholder's meetings, and the like, and the remaining third from printing catalogs, brochures, fliers, and other miscellaneous printing jobs. Largely because securities are high-value-added items that do not cost much to print, annual sales are about ¥1.6 billion ($6.3 million).

Asia Printing decided to implement NPS methods because Morio Ueno, its president, knew Mikiya Kinoshita. Ueno had heard that NPS was very effective and asked Kinoshita to come and take a look at his company. Recalling the day that instructors from NPS visited his company, Ueno says he was as shocked as if he had been struck by a hammer when one told him he was surprised that Asia Printing had not gone bankrupt already. The instructor added: "What are you doing? You are in a made-to-order industry. You print only after receiving an order from a customer. Why do you have such a big inventory of paper?"

Walking through the factory, the instructor would point to a worker and ask: "Is he doing some value-adding task? What do you think?" Ueno had nothing to say when an instructor said:

> The only time that a printer adds value is when he or she is actually printing. Watching a printing press print does not add value. I see workers stacking and unstacking

paper, but why don't you think of a way to eliminate the stacking and the unstacking? If your customer pays you for stacking and unstacking the paper, then you can do it. The worker will only experience the joy of working when he or she is doing something a customer will pay for. It is inhuman to make an employee work diligently at a task that has no social value.

Starting with Shorter Lead Time

Ueno decided to implement the NPS methods and set, as his initial goals, reducing lead time and improving quality control. Lead time, in the printing business, refers to the time that elapses from receipt of the original copy from a customer until delivery of the final product, printed and bound. The shorter the lead time, the more competitive the printer. Securities and financial reports are printed under very strict deadlines. A missed delivery deadline can have serious consequences. For example, a notice of a stockholders' meeting must be sent out two weeks prior to the meeting. If the notice is even one day late, the meeting becomes invalid. Financial reports frequently require numerous corrections, which take time to make. A printed financial report may even have to be discarded because a phrase must be changed here and there. It is also very easy to make a numerical mistake in a financial report.

For these reasons, a short lead time is vitally important for the business. Customers want the printed matter to be delivered on time and without mistakes. The continued survival of a printer depends on satisfying that need — something easier said than done.

After implementing NPS methods, Asia Printing's lead time was cut in half in less than two years. With rush jobs, it is now possible to receive copy in the afternoon and deliver the final printed product the following morning.

With the reduced lead time, more and more jobs are being referred to Asia Printing from other printers who cannot meet a delivery deadline. A frequent request is to print documents related to stockholders' meetings that cannot be printed in time by other printers.

Reducing the lead time began with finding the bottleneck — determining which of the production processes had the lowest throughput. Among phototypesetting, proofing, plate making, printing, and bookbinding, increasing the throughput of the slowest task made the entire job flow more smoothly.

When a process with a greater throughput overrides a slower rate-determining process and continues to pass its own output downstream, the quantity of work-in-process increases unchecked. Once the bottleneck process is identified and improved, the overall throughput increases, the job flow improves, and the quantity of work-in-process decreases. When the throughput of each process becomes the same, it is easier to predict the amount of time that it will take from receipt of original copy to completion of the end product.

Another important requirement in reducing lead time is shortening the set-up time for each process. For example, if the set-up time required for a job is 40 minutes, reducing it to 10 or even 5 minutes invariably improves the production flow.

If a salesman receives copy from a customer but leaves it sitting on his desk for a half a day before passing it along to production, that wasted half-day has to be included in the lead time. It is necessary to reduce the time that copy or a plate is kept in the waiting mode.

When a salesman receives original copy, it must be delivered promptly to the production floor. Production floor workers must prepare a plate, which must then be proofed and, if necessary, corrected. It is important to eliminate any waiting time from the process. The key to reducing the lead time is to create a system that accomplishes this. The set-up time affects not only how quickly a printing press can be started but also how quickly the printed matter can be delivered to the bindery.

Leveling Production and Reducing Customer Inventory

Reducing the lead time produced an unexpected benefit for Asia Printing. The unit price charged by a printer usually goes down as the number of printed copies increases. For example, the price per copy is usually less for 10,000 copies than for 500. The reason is that printing more copies with one setup increases the efficiency of the operation, hence reduces the unit price.

However when the set-up time is reduced, for example, from 40 minutes to 10 minutes, it is possible to tell a customer that the unit price is the same whether you print, for example, 10,000 or 2,000. A customer frequently decides to print 10,000 copies because the unit price is lower than for printing 2,000. Many unused copies end up lying around in a customer's warehouse. Catalogs and the like are frequently reprinted since the old catalogs contain out-of-date information. The already printed catalogs are wasted, which is one reason you see catalogs with pasted-in correction strips.

Asia Printing's policy is to prevent its customers from having to keep or discard inventory. Asia Printing calls this policy the *stockless method*. When Asia Printing receives an order for 10,000 copies, it initially prints only the immediately needed number, for example, 2,000. Asia Printing tells the customer that the order for the remaining 8,000 is on hold and will be delivered when they become needed. With this method, corrections requested by a customer are easily incorporated. Plates or films can be corrected before the remaining pieces are printed, and the customers receive printed matter incorporating the latest information. The customers do not have to carry an inventory and the warehouse cost is reduced.

The advantage of the stockless method for Asia Printing is that the work load is leveled. When large orders must be handled all at once, smaller jobs are kept waiting. However, when 2,000 copies are handled in each lot instead of 10,000 copies, five jobs can be processed in the same amount of time.

Success in the Disclosure Business

The printing industry is highly competitive. It is said that Dai Nippon Printing and Toppan Printing earn 70 to 80 percent of their profit from business lines not directly related to printing, such as electronics. Indeed, the profitability of printers such as Kyodo Printing and Tosho Printing, which were slow to diversify into electronics, is poor. Against this backdrop, Asia Printing is developing a way for a printer to survive as an information business. Asia Printing calls this the "disclosure business."

Because it prints securities, Asia Printing has numerous business contacts. Taking advantage of this, Asia Printing has developed a full-service business in printing all kinds of documents related to a company's financial reports. In other words, Asia Printing is now printing balance sheets, capital-increase notices for filing with the Ministry of Finance, documents to be filed when listing a company on the stock exchange, special reports to be published when issuing bonds overseas, and the like. The company has hired a group of specialists to assist customers in determining their documentation requirements. Asia Printing also holds seminars for customers, all of which are designed to increase its customer base.

These strategies and the benefits of the stockless method are expected to result in a rapid increase in Asia Printing's business. At the present time, Asia Printing has business relations with 400 listed companies. Ueno expects Asia Printing to expand the number of listed companies it does business with by 50 to 60 companies per year. Ueno also hopes to annually increase Asia Printing's sales by at least 25 percent. Though Asia Securities Printing is still a small printer, Ueno is confident that it will soon become large enough to be listed on the stock exchange.

PART THREE

Conversations with the Top Executives of NPS

CHAPTER ELEVEN

A Conversation with Kikuo Suzumura, Chairman of the Implementation Committee

*W*HY DOES *a company that introduces the NPS methods change quickly into a super-high-profitability company? We'd like to learn what the essence of NPS is from the chairman of the Implementation Committee.*

Suzumura: We don't do anything special. There are more disbelievers than believers in our philosophy. NPS is a group of believers in our philosophy, people determined to survive while others go bankrupt. There is no need for nonmembers to understand what we are trying to do.

We've heard that NPS tells its members not to mass-produce, that they have to produce what is demanded, when it is demanded, and at the same low cost as in mass production.

Suzumura: The important thing is how you understand the present age, whether you believe the age of high economic growth will continue or not.

The post-World War II era was one of shortages in Japan. Demand totally outstripped supply. Following the mid-1960s, the rate of increase in demand started to slow down, and supply began to increase faster than demand. We call the period when demand outstripped supply the *Pattern-A age* and the period when supply outstripped demand the *Pattern-B age.*

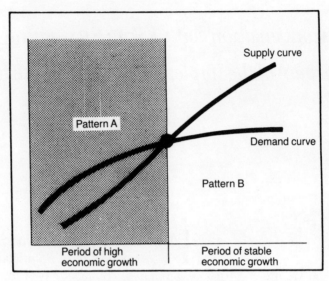

Figure 6. Pattern-A and Pattern-B Production

After the onset of the Pattern-B age, we were fortunate that excess supply could be exported and that there was no domestic oversupply of goods. However, as exports increased, trade friction became a problem with all products — textiles, iron and steel, automobiles, and so on. For the exporting nation, free trade and increasing exports are fine. But for the importing nation, excessive imports become a problem that cannot be ignored. It means unemployment and balance-of-payment problems.

Japan, a nation without natural resources, must earn foreign currency. It must export — and it must be careful how it exports. It is one thing to drive at 45 miles per hour when the posted speed limit is 40. But if you drive 20 or 30 miles per hour above the speed limit, you are going to get caught. In trade, this is equivalent to charges of dumping and the specter of trade friction. Sixty percent of our automobile production is exported. Only 40 percent is sold domestically. No wonder there is a problem.

At any rate, during the Pattern-A age, manufacturers just produced. Producing more meant more profits. Even if something didn't sell today, it sold eventually, a month later or six months later. What NPS is saying is that this is no longer true.

Market Determines Price in the Pattern-B Age

Is NPS saying that in this age of oversupply, the old beliefs no longer apply?

Suzumura: It is important to use a system and a method that allows supply to fit demand. When technological innovation occurs so quickly, overproducing usually hastens obsolescence and an inability to respond to price-cutting by competitors. Large-scale integrated circuits, hand-held calculators, and digital watches are good examples.

However, there still is a common belief that "big is good." There is still a belief that mass-production improves efficiency and productivity.

The notion of profit is also defined incorrectly. It is a mistake to think that the difference between selling price and total cost represents a company's profit. Yoshihiro Inayama, former chairman of Nippon Steel, used to say: "The price of iron is equal to the sum of the costs plus a reasonable profit." He was describing how the selling price should be determined (some call this the "logic of iron"). But when you think about it, the selling price should be determined in the marketplace.

In the Pattern-A age, it made sense to say that the "selling price is equal to cost plus a reasonable profit." In the Pattern-B age, nobody will accept such a thing. However, even in this age, many people still believe in the old idea. It is almost comical. People still believe that profit increases when you mass-produce and reduce cost.

That belief is correct, if you can sell everything you produce. However, name me a product in this age that can be sold in any quantity at the price set by the manufacturer. Any product may sell well in the beginning, but excessive production always ends up undermining prices. That's why NPS says mass production is not the only production method, that it can even have dire consequences.

Why Inventory Increases When Goods Are Selling Well

Suzumura: There are many ways of improving efficiency. For example, if 10 workers produce 100 items a day and if new equipment allows the same 10 workers to produce 120 items a day, efficiency has gone up 20 percent. If all the products can be sold, the increased efficiency is fine. But if the increased production results in products remaining unsold, then the efficiency of the company as a whole has gone down. Another way of increasing efficiency is to produce 100 items with 8 workers instead of 10 workers. This is also a 20 percent increase in efficiency.

Do you fire the two surplus workers?

Suzumura: It is totally unacceptable to fire workers who become superfluous as efficiency improves. This is betraying your colleagues. What you do is employ them to fabricate in-house what you used to subcontract out.

Presently there is a surplus of workers. Every company has its "unemployed employees." There is probably nothing more painful for a human being than not being able to devote him or herself to productive work. Companies used to hire people almost indiscriminately and now they are virtually killing them off. This is intolerable.

There would be no superfluous workers if a company had been working to achieve the most with the smallest possible number of workers. Moreover, if it has superfluous workers, it should use those workers to produce in-house what was sub-

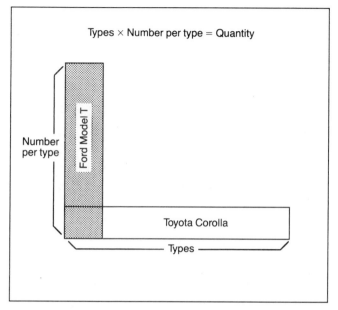

Figure 7. Horizontal and Vertical Production

contracted out. There is no justification for writing those workers off and assigning them to dead-end jobs. Nor is it acceptable from the worker's perspective to give a person some meaningless task just to keep him or her from being idle. Each of us has only one life to live. Just because a worker is being paid does not give a company the right to make that person work at tasks that are of no value. Doing that is nothing more than dereliction of duty on the part of management.

Companies are overburdened not only with people but also with inventory.

Suzumura: Take, for example, automobiles. Ford used to manufacture only Model Ts. They didn't produce many models, but they sold large quantities of the same model. Figure 7 illustrates the equation:

Quantity = number of models × number of cars per model.

In the figure, this quantity is represented as an "area." Since only a few models were produced, the area of the Model T was very tall. In the late seventies, according to one study, Toyota was producing about 75,000 Corollas a month with approximately 350 different body types. This meant that the number produced per model was small and that the area was very wide but low in height.

In the coming age of high-diversity, small-lot production, the quantity area will become flat for every company. Even though the management of most companies may understand this in theory, however, they behave as if they still believed in low-diversity mass production.

What happens is this: Companies report that they're making good profits. But when you look into their profit picture, you notice that sales and profits are increasing but so are debts and inventory. That is nonsense.

How can inventory increase when you are selling well? If goods are selling, inventory must decrease. With most companies, they don't think it strange that sales, profits, inventory, and debts are all increasing at the same time. Now, I do find this strange.

Kikuo Suzumura

Learning from a Sushi Restaurant

How should production operate?

Suzumura: We say: "Learn from the sushi restaurants." At a sushi restaurant, the chef never says: "Who wants tuna? Who wants cucumber rolls?" The chef never takes the initiative or forces a choice on the diners. The customer always asks for what he or she wants, whether it's shrimp, squid, or whatever, and the chef prepares it on the spot. If a sushi restaurant served only tuna, nobody would eat there.

Manufacturers, however, tend to produce what they want to produce and then expect customers to buy it. Even if a manufacturer is producing three items, A, B, and C, it will, in the name of greater efficiency, mass-produce A, then B, and then C.

You mean production in lots.

Suzumura: Yes. Suppose that products A, B, and C are selling on the market but that the manufacturer wants to produce A this month, B the next month, and C the following month. The manufacturer must then have a supply of all three products at the same time. It would have to predict the inventory level required for the next three months and then produce on the basis of those predictions. What are you going to do if your prediction is wrong, which it invariably is?

It is better to produce A, B, and C every day. In other words, the basic production method must be to produce in the smallest lot size, that is, one at a time.

There is a hidden trap in thinking that it is more efficient and less costly to mass-produce A, then B, and so on.

Suzumura: With the traditional production method, it was not possible to produce C if there was a shortage of C. You had to produce A and B first. However, if you produce A, B, and C in small lots, you can stop producing A and produce C first. You can produce C first, then B, then A, for example. This means that you can produce what is needed and avoid producing what is not needed. You may be producing the same number of goods overall, but the production mix will vary.

As an example, think of a rice cooker with a 1-quart capacity. A person cooking for a family of four may make only half that amount; if each family member eats a half cup of rice, all the rice that is cooked will be eaten. However, if the capacity of the rice cooker is one quart, you tend to cook one quart. You think you're saving money because the cost of electricity per half quart of rice is less if you cook a whole quart rather than a half. But what about the leftover rice?

Modern rice cookers conveniently keep the rice warm. The rice you cook for dinner remains warm even the following morning. Keeping the rice warm consumes electricity. Moreover, in the morning, the parents may instead drink milk and eat bread and rush off to work. The children don't eat much because they'll be late for school. So in the morning only about half of the leftover rice is eaten, with one cup remaining. Someone may eat some of it for lunch, but there's still some left to be kept warm until dinner. The electricity bill keeps rising, and eventually the leftover rice is thrown away.

With a company, expenses are divided into many items like production cost, administrative cost, and transportation cost. A decrease of one cost can be easily offset by increased spending on some other item. As a result, companies are spending money in a manner that is tantamount to throwing the money away.

Beware of Opportunity Loss

The most important thing for a company is to create a system that does not produce waste.

Suzumura: You've heard the term "opportunity loss." Opportunity loss occurs when you don't have a product that could have been sold if you had had it. This is a stupid term. There is no loss. You just didn't make the profit.

In poker, if you fold immediately, you haven't lost anything. You just didn't win. But if you stay in the game till the end and then lose, you lose all the bets you made throughout. If you fold quickly and someone else wins the hand, you don't win the bets, so this is opportunity loss. But you don't lose chips unless you stay in the game until the end.

Another misleading term is "investment in inventory." How can inventory be an investment? Something is out of focus. "Investment in inventory" is a reflection of Pattern-A thinking, where you believe that your inventory will always eventually be sold.

What I find strange these days are the book publishers. I am told that bookstores return many unsold books to the publishers. I don't know why these publishers persist in their foolish practice.

For example, if a publisher thinks that 10,000 copies of a 110-page book can be sold, the publisher will print 10,000 copies of the first signature (a group of pages printed on one sheet), then 10,000 copies of the second signature, then 10,000 copies of the third signature, and so on until 10,000 copies of the last signature are printed. A book becomes available for the first time then. Because of this practice, the printing press is running at a frantic pace in the beginning while the bookbinding operation is idle. Ten thousand books are printed and then delivered to bookstores. If the books don't sell, they are returned. Why do the publishers engage in such a practice?

A better way would be to print each signature in lots of a thousand. You print 1,000 copies of the first signature, 1,000 copies of the second, and so on. After 1,000 copies of the final signature are printed, you deliver all of the signatures to the bookbinder. You then repeat the entire process, printing 1,000 copies of each signature. While that is going on, the bookbinder has produced 1,000 completed books.

The books are delivered to the bookstores, and you keep track of how well they sell. You deliver the next 1,000 books to the bookstores. By the time you've sold 2,000 or 3,000 books, you have a good idea of how well the book is selling. If you thought that 10,000 books would sell but they don't do as well as you thought, you can stop publishing after 4,000 or 5,000 books. This would eliminate most of the problems with returned books.

If you think the book will sell, just continue producing in lots of 1,000, ten times so that you have 10,000 books. If you think it will sell more, you can repeat the process. The publisher will make more profit if fewer books are returned. Worrying doesn't make the books sell well. I criticize the publishers often, but they never seem to learn.

The problem with printing presses is changing the setup. Printers say that changing the printing plates requires set-up time. The answer is to reduce the set-up time. The printers want to print 10,000 copies once the setup is completed. If publishers keep listening to what the printers say, publishers will strangle themselves.

The only requirement is to produce frequently in small lots. Unless you change the production practice, the sales practice won't change either. This NPS's basic belief.

More Time Spent Waiting than Producing

What are your views regarding investment in machinery and other equipment?

Suzumura: A robot is only a tool. It is not omnipotent. In the old days, when a samurai on horseback had to fight many opponents on open ground, he used a weapon called a *jin tachi*. If he had to fight a single opponent on foot, he used the conventional Japanese sword. If he had to fight indoors, he used a *sho tachi*. If he had to engage in hand-to-hand combat, he used a *yoroi toshi*. The samurai used weapons that suited the situation. There is no need to use a fancy Japanese sword to cut vegetables. A simple kitchen knife will do. It is important to select the most efficient tool for the purpose, the tool that requires the smallest investment. The vegetables will taste the same whether it is sliced with an ordinary kitchen knife or a legendary Japanese sword made by a master craftsman. But remember that the cost per slice of vegetable is prohibitively expensive if you slice it with a Japanese sword costing thousands of dollars. Many people nevertheless persist in thinking that cutting vegetables using a sword made by a master craftsman will increase the value of the vegetable.

You are saying that people incorrectly assume that using the latest equipment will produce a better product and that modern equipment leads to greater efficiency.

Suzumura: The term *lead time* refers to the time spent producing a piece of merchandise, that is, the time from when the raw materials are fed into the system until the end product is delivered to a customer. However, those on the production floor do not understand that the lead time includes not only the time spent actually producing the item but also the time during which nothing is being done to it, the time it spends just waiting. Those in production try to install equipment that processes goods faster. But they don't realize that the time spent before and after processing is usually much longer than the processing time itself.

For example, consider how much time is spent hammering, sawing, planing, and so on in building a house. It may take only one day to build the framework of a modest home. But the entire construction period may take two to three months. Why is that? That's because so much time is wasted with materials just lying around. When someone suggests shortening the construction time, people just look at minor details, trying to shave off a little time here and there. They don't try to change the system. You must remember that the important thing is not the equipment used but the flow of goods.

I know people will object when I say this. But take, for example, a flexible manufacturing system (FMS). An FMS is like a mixed tenant building in which the raw ingredients are the tenants. When a button is pressed, the desired product is produced. An FMS is valuable only because there is no system that can produce what is necessary when it is necessary. An FMS is not truly flexible. If you manufacture something and then just store it, there is no capital turnover.

Managers Should Not Become Time Thieves

Faced with an age of slow economic growth, many companies are investing heavily in research and development (R & D), trying to diversify. At the same time, companies are realizing how expensive R & D is. What are NPS's views toward R & D?

Suzumura: Research and development involves a lot of trial and error. It is costly. Therefore, R & D funds must be generated internally using the existing system. Many companies borrow money from a bank to fund an R & D program for developing a new product. If the R & D effort does not produce any concrete results, what have you accomplished with the borrowed money? The important thing is to make sure that the existing business generates a profit. Your own funds can then be used to finance R & D or whatever. Of course it is important not to be left behind. Even if the batting average is .100, you still need to try. But an indispensable condition is to use your own funds.

To fund an R & D program using borrowed money is nothing but a gamble. When you gamble with money borrowed from a loan shark, you can end up losing not only the game but your life or your family's life as well.

If you gamble using your own pocket money, the most you'll have to do after losing will be to not go out for a few days. In other words, there's nothing risky about R & D if what you do is cut waste from the present system and use the money you saved to fund the program or to invest it in some other way. If you stop engaging in R & D simply because most R & D efforts are fruitless, you'll certainly be left behind. A new challenge is always accompanied by failures and difficulties. Failures and difficulties can produce unexpected results.

Nevertheless, there is no end to the number of companies that gamble on a new product or a capital investment and end up bankrupt.

Suzumura: It is okay for the owner of a business to take a chance and fail. The owner is just being responsible. The tragedy is for the employees who get caught up in the mistake. Employees believe in the company president and follow loyally. If products manufactured by employees using their precious time end up being discounted or sold for next to nothing, this means the company president has stolen the employees' irreplaceable time. If you steal money or goods, you get sent to jail as a thief. But nothing happens when you steal employees' time. You can buy goods, but you can't buy time. Once it's gone, it's gone. Company presidents must not forget that they are borrowing employees' time. I'm saying that company presidents must not steal employees' time. A president might say, "Don't complain. I'm paying your salary." But it is still employee abuse. The employees' wages do not come out of the company president's pocket. The wages can be paid only because the workers are working for the company. A company president who says such a thing is totally wrong.

It's useless to waste words on those who can't understand. In NPS, we simply try to teach the basics to our members.

CHAPTER TWELVE

A Conversation with
Director Mikiya Kinoshita

*T*HE NPS *Research Association was founded in January 1981. Why did you have a gag rule until 1985, telling your members that disclosing anything about NPS to nonmembers would result in expulsion?*

Kinoshita: Because of our rule to admit as a member only one company from each industry, we tried to remain unknown. With the "one industry, one company rule," we would have to deny admission to late comers from an industry that is already represented. However, in many cases, friends and acquaintances are interested, and it is difficult to say no to them. Also, we didn't want unnecessary attention. Those are the reasons that we tried to keep a low profile.

I also avoided interviews and meeting people. However, as the number of member companies increased, it became impossible to stop leaks of information about us. Also, when a company's financial condition improves and people ask why, it is difficult to explain how it happened. For these reasons, we've loosened the gag rule so now a member can talk a little bit about NPS.

Who was the first to suggest creating an association such as NPS?

Kinoshita: It wasn't me. The suggestion came from Hoashi, president of Kibun, and Azuma, president of Oiresu, and

others. I was ill at that time so I was limited in giving advice
and so on. I wasn't aggressively involved in the beginning.

What was the motive for forming the NPS Research Association?

Kinoshita: I wanted to leave a philosophy for posterity, a philosophy that described how manufacturing ought to be done.
We are looking for companies that are willing to go so far as to
include the NPS philosophy in their articles of incorporation.

*Why do you want your philosophy included in a company's articles
of incorporation?*

Kinoshita: We are looking for companies that are so committed to management based on the NPS philosophy that they
don't mind doing that.

*Your member companies tend to be headed by presidents who own
the company — sole proprietorships.*

Kinoshita: It has turned out that way. I was surprised when
I found this out recently, but 95 percent of Japanese companies
are headed by hired presidents. When we go to companies
headed by hired presidents and tell these executives what
they're doing is wrong, that they have to shape up, they usually complain that they are being embarrassed in front of the
employees, that they have nowhere to go. They don't feel that

Mikihiro Kinoshita

they must put up with a little embarrassment for the good of the company. These presidents are only concerned about their job security or their image.

Owner-presidents, on the other hand, don't worry about criticism. If we criticize them, they'll challenge us. They're more driven. I think those are the reasons that our member companies tend to be run by owner-presidents.

How does NPS differ from other consultants?

Kinoshita: Simply put, with ordinary consultants, regardless of whether a company came to the consultant or the consultant sought out the company, the consultant promises to do something, and a contract is signed if the client accepts the promise. It doesn't work that way with us. We tell the president of a company seeking membership to visit a member company and to see firsthand what is being done. Once the president is satisfied that what the member company is doing is what the president's own company needs, we then consider that company for membership. This is an important point.

Because we are seeking companies that will pass along our philosophy to posterity, we make sure the president is truly committed to NPS.

We don't need to involve uninterested parties. If other companies believe in TQC (total quality control) as their basic philosophy, that's fine. We are a group that believes the NPS philosophy is the best.

A Bond Based on Comradeship

A company cannot join NPS, then, simply by paying a membership fee?

Kinoshita: No. At the very least, the company president must come to us seeking membership. We talk with him, and we don't start working with him until we have formed a bond based on comradeship.

If the president sincerely hopes to become a member and we are convinced that he is truly committed, we then visit his company to ascertain the potential and future of the company. If we're satisfied, we get involved.

Is the membership fee high?

Kinoshita: No. Our purpose is not to make money. Our objective is to nurture companies that will pass along our philosophy to posterity. Some even ask us why the membership fee is so low. There are three monthly fee levels: ¥500,000 ($2,000), ¥800,000 ($3,200), and ¥1.2 million ($4,800). We do not charge any fee for the first six or twelve months if a company does not reach a point that satisfies us. We bear all the costs, and we do not allow formal membership until we're satisfied with the company's progress. We don't ask for a fee until membership is granted. So everything is free until then.

Is the one major difference between NPS and other consultants the fact that NPS does not seek profits?

Kinoshita: Yes. We don't consider it a business. The NPS Research Association is backed up by a company called MIP. The stockholders of MIP are the member companies of NPS. This means that any profit made by NPS belongs to the members. All the profits are pooled.

What is the capital of MIP?

Kinoshita: It's now ¥127 million ($505,000).

You mentioned passing NPS's philosophy along to posterity. What exactly is this philosophy?

Kinoshita: A manufacturer buys raw materials and sells finished products. It is imperative for the manufacturer to meet the customer's requirements as to quality, cost, and delivery time. All factors that hamper meeting those goals are considered waste. Our basic philosophy is the total elimination of waste.

Things that increase costs, for example inventory, interest, and unnecessary equipment, are all examples of waste. How can we eliminate waste? There are, of course, many ways.

How many instructors does NPS itself employ?

Kinoshita: Currently about 11.

There are now about 30 member companies. Will that number increase?

Kinoshita: I don't know how people hear about us. But we get so many requests for help. Once you meet somebody, it's hard to say no. So I try not to meet people.

How many companies have been denied membership?

Kinoshita: About 300. There are also quite a few companies with applications currently pending.

How many companies can you help?

Kinoshita: I think about 300. With our current resources, we can handle about 100. So the maximum is probably about three times our current capacity.

Do your current members want the membership to increase?

Kinoshita: The members believe that things are working well enough now and they worry that increasing the membership will weaken the group's solidarity. I fear most that the Association could lose its sense of unity. I don't decide whether a membership application is accepted or rejected. We require a recommendation by two member companies and approval by all the members.

The number of instructors you have trained in the member companies is increasing. Do you employ instructors on a subcontract basis?

Kinoshita: Yes. We have a pool of about 100 individuals with the ability to serve as instructors. We expect that number to increase quickly.

Improvements Are Evident from the First Day

I hear that the instructors are pretty strict. I've been told that an instructor actually kicked one plant manager.

Kinoshita: If you're not diligent, that's possible. But as long as you're diligent, there's no danger. However, many people aren't serious. We do our best for the company, but some people don't really care.

They look at you, wondering why you're there.

Kinoshita: With NPS, the president of every member company has studied the NPS method and is committed to it. Even so, there may be directors or plant managers who remain uncommitted. When we see that, we tell them they are disobeying the president's order. They are not doing what the president tells them to do. I think that's terrible.

I find many disagreeable people sent to companies by banks. They think they are the watchdogs for their bank. They don't want to work. It's also the bank's fault. A bank may notice that a company is about to go bankrupt. But the bank still charges high interest and has the audacity to send an overseer to the company. I think it's about time for banks to reconsider their behavior.

When a company accepts NPS methods, how long does it take before business visibly improves?

Kinoshita: Improvements occur from the first day. Space may be freed up, or fewer workers may be needed. Benefits are seen the first day. However, it takes about two years for the "pupil" to finish kindergarten and enter first grade.

This is true of any company, but the quantity of work-in-process and the inventory decrease, and receivables are collected sooner. It's difficult to collect payment when you are forcing your products onto your customers. They're more willing to pay when you sell them only what they need. It's easier to do that when you produce only as much as can be sold. Everything turns for the worse when you accumulate inventory.

The World Company only produces what can be sold. There's no need to discount. You're in trouble if you have to discount in order to sell.

In any company, the marketing and sales departments make a big fuss if they lose any sales. But they don't care if a huge inventory is created because they couldn't sell what was produced.

With NPS member companies listed on the stock exchange, does the stock price reflect the company's improved financial condition?

Kinoshita: The financial condition of NPS members does improve. This may have a minor positive effect on the stock price. But that is not our objective. Our objective is to make a company more efficient.

Is the NPS method an application of Kanban or the Toyota production system?

Kinoshita: We are involved not only with production. We call the NPS method a management philosophy. A manufacturer cannot concern itself only with the production system. It must receive orders from customers, deliver the products, and collect payment. It's meaningless to criticize only the plant operations.

The ideal business practice is similar to that of a noodle shop. At a noodle shop, the customer places an order, the cook prepares the dish, and the store owner collects the bill. There are no accounts receivable. You only have to be a diligent worker. A well-run noodle shop reflects not only an efficient way of preparing noodles but also an efficient way of running a business. NPS is concerned not only with streamlining the production departments. We accept as members only those companies willing to accept the NPS philosophy as the company's overall business philosophy.

In other words, you provide instruction that pertains not only to production but also to finances, accounting, and sales?

Kinoshita: Yes, because our concern is to make management more efficient, we do that. We teach the company how to create a system. With manufacturers, more than half — actually 80 percent — of the work by the sales and marketing departments involves claims processing for defective merchandise and keeping track of scheduled deliveries. So if the production departments can ensure quality and timely delivery, sales and marketing won't have much to do. But actually, that's when the true job of the marketing and sales department begins. If the R & D department suggests developing some product, existing equipment will be used first. Once it's confirmed that the product will sell, a small line can be created. If the product sells, the idea is to find the next thing to produce.

Subcontracting Is Not Cheap

As production becomes more efficient, fewer workers are needed. In sales, it's possible for a worker to be transferred to some other sales activity. But what do you do with surplus production workers? Wait for them to quit?

Kinoshita: The NPS method is not a method for firing workers. We do not ask workers to work hard so that their colleagues can be fired. That is inhuman. We say, "No firing." We also say, "Do not hire a new worker when a worker quits." When you hire workers, women included, you have to be willing to keep them for a lifetime.

Anyway, all companies use subcontractors for many different jobs. The surplus workers can be easily absorbed by fabricating in house what was previously subcontracted out. The reason is that surplus workers are created gradually, not all at once.

That can also reduce unwanted friction with subcontractors.

Kinoshita: Some subcontractors have many subcontracting relationships so that the termination of a business relationship with one company is compensated by new relationships. It's a case-by-case situation.

With high-diversity, small-lot production, it seems like subcontracting might be cheaper. You're saying that that's not necessarily the case.

Kinoshita: The members of NPS think that's not the case. However, most people still believe that subcontracting is cheaper and that mass-production reduces cost.

We believe that subcontracting is more expensive than in-house fabrication. We also say: "Don't mass-produce. Produce only as much as needed. Use high-diversity, small-lot short-production-time manufacturing methods to produce goods at the same cost as that of mass-production."

When faced with a need for high-diversity, small-lot production, many companies force their subcontractors to comply. The subcontracting company does the easy part. What then happens is that the subcontractor gains the ability to perform high-diversity, small-lot production. The subcontracting company doesn't gain the broader production experience.

You're saying this is detrimental in the long run.

Kinoshita: Yes, I think so. When you're a manufacturer, you must do the hard work. It's better to contract out the easy jobs and to produce in-house the parts that require frequent setup changes, the difficult parts.

This is the reverse of conventional wisdom.

Kinoshita: Yes, and I think I'm right. I tell the members that it's as if you ordered out for sushi every time you expected guests for dinner. After five or ten years you would know the telephone numbers of all the sushi restaurants, but you wouldn't know how to cook.

Not Carrying Inventory

Kinoshita: For the continued survival of a country such as Japan — a small country with limited resources — it is important to use high-diversity, small-lot production methods in order to produce quickly only what can be sold. During the period of high economic growth in Japan, demand outstripped supply. This meant that what was produced would eventually be sold. This is no longer the case.

What most companies do when faced with this situation is to produce five or ten different varieties instead of only one variety as in the past. But sales don't increase. Moreover, customers demand that goods be delivered immediately. What then happens is that the producer maintains an inventory of a wide variety of goods, that is, both the depth and breadth of its inventory increase. The error in this method is that the producer tries to meet orders by shipping goods from inventory. What the producer should be doing is meeting the orders by manufacturing what is ordered. This eliminates inventory. That's what we are trying to do. You shouldn't maintain an inventory.

You're saying that maintaining an inventory is bad.

Kinoshita: Yes. However, some items have to be kept in inventory because of their seasonal nature. But there is a difference between a planned and an unplanned inventory.

Some people refer to the NPS method as the Toyota system or kanban method. They're wrong. You have to be concerned with the overall efficiency of the entire company. There's no sense in producing at a low cost if the company goes bankrupt.

We're told that NPS tells its members not to invest in equipment and machinery.

Kinoshita: No. Capital investment is fine. The problem is how much equipment and machinery you invest in. There is a big difference between installing the equipment required to produce what can be sold and installing equipment with a capacity that may be needed in the future when production increases five- or tenfold. You must invest in equipment that fits current sales. You have to realize that almost all forecasts miss the mark. So, NPS tells its members over and over not to invest in equipment on the basis of predicted future sales.

You must not invest in machines that are capable of mass-producing only one thing. What are you going to do if the product doesn't sell? If the equipment is versatile enough to produce different things, then there's no problem.

How NPS Has Changed Member Companies

The first company that joined NPS was Oiresu. Can you tell me specifically what sort of company it is and what changes have taken place?

Kinoshita: Oiresu is a leading manufacturer of oil-free bearings. It is a good company with a strong R & D orientation. It develops new materials and creates new needs. It formerly relied heavily on subcontractors to come up with the end products.

When we first inspected the company, our assessment was that its R & D and sales capabilities were fine but that its production capabilities were almost nonexistent. We thought that Oiresu would become invulnerable if it developed proper production capabilities. What we did was to start in-house fabrication, line by line, not everything at once. This improved Oiresu's production capability and profitability.

With Kibun, you changed the production process layout. What changes resulted?

Kinoshita: This is true of all companies, not just Kibun. When a company buys a machine from a manufacturer, it uses the machine as supplied by the manufacturer, without modifying it to suit its own requirements. At Kibun, we modified their machines to suit their own requirements.

A company like Kibun that produces perishable foodstuffs must supply the freshest possible products. This means it is best to produce only after an order is received. At the same time, one must improve the yield and turnover rate and not tolerate any defective merchandise.

As far as delivery was concerned, Kibun used to ship all its products to a central distribution center, from which they were then delivered to retail stores. We told Kibun to stop doing such a stupid thing and instead to deliver directly to their customers once final processing was completed. This improved freshness and cut cost.

Can you describe the changes at Asahi Tokushu Gohan Company? We understand that the plywood industry is in the midst of a recession.

Kinoshita: The same thing happened there. Customers are selfish so they want a diversity of products and immediate delivery. To meet these needs, Asahi built one warehouse after another. That's a quick path to bankruptcy. We told Asahi to stop doing this, to produce only after an order had been received. We had a big argument over that. Salespeople feel secure where there is an inventory. They go out and sell with confidence. We told them that they were wrong, that they had to sell the products from the catalog, and that the orders they got would be filled without a hitch. Things have changed quite a bit.

An asbestos slate manufacturing company called Nozawa has changed its system so that not even one slate is kept in inventory. This turned a loss-ridden company into a profitable one.

Can you describe the company Ogura Hoseki Seiki?

Kinoshita: That company manufactures phonograph needles. Ogura used to manufacture needles in lots of 2,000. Now they produce in lots of 20. When the needles were being produced in lots of 2,000, the finished lots would be subjected to a random inspection. If a defect was found in any of the needles, all 2,000 — the entire lot — were discarded. With a lot size of 20, the most you have to discard at once is 20. The ideal would be to produce in lots of one. That would be the safest and most efficient method.

Akai Electric is still facing difficulties. The VTR market is a very tough one, and that doesn't help. However, we have reduced the lot size from 2,000 units to 50.

It Is Best to Produce in Units of One

Kinoshita: Our member companies come from different industries, but they all have one feature in common. The essential goal is to produce in a lot size of one. With Misawa Homes, that meant one house at a time. It would be best if all the parts required to build a single house were produced one item at a time and would all come together at the end. Misawa Homes used to believe incorrectly that it was cheaper to produce the elements of ten homes at a time.

The traditional way to manufacture clothing is to produce all the collars at one time, then the sleeves, and so on. The parts would be sewn together at the end. But it is better to finish one garment at a time, as World does. That's all there is to it. World can produce most articles of clothing in two days, whereas it takes a month with other companies. World can afford to produce only after an order has been received from a retail shop.

Until now the method you just described would have been thought inefficient.

Kinoshita: Watch how a housekeeper cooks at home. She turns on the rice cooker, brews the tea, broils the fish, prepares the soup, and tosses the salad all at the same time in the right sequence. That's what I'm talking about. Having done this so many times, housekeepers no longer have to think about it.

But with companies, almost all of them have on hand one or two months' worth of inventory. It's as if they had a month's supply of cooked rice and soup. Then they panic, claiming that they don't have enough broiled fish. This is the situation at most companies. What do you think? If you would produce only what can be sold today, you would need fewer workers, less equipment, less warehouse space, and fewer managers.

When one looks at a company from this perspective, one's view changes as to how the R & D, administrative, accounting, and finance departments should operate. The presidents of all the NPS member companies are aware of this. But most other company presidents are not aware of it.

Many of your member companies are not listed on the stock exchange. Do you plan to have these companies go public in the future?

Kinoshita: Yes. I hope all our member companies will go public. I hope to see companies listed on the second stock exchange move up to the first. When one's company is not listed, it is difficult to hire the right people. When all is said and done, the quality of a company depends on the quality of its people. It is very important to hire capable people.

CHAPTER THIRTEEN

——————

A Conversation with the
Supreme Advisor, Taiichi Ohno

E VEN *though it is said that we*
have entered the age of low and
stable economic growth, many companies still believe in mass produc-
tion and mass sales. They invest aggressively in equipment and
machinery and suffer later from overproduction and excess capacity.

Ohno: We often say that anyone can cut costs with low-
diversity mass production — this method is fine, as long as
you can sell everything you produce. But if you have to discount to sell what you produce, you won't make money. What
good does it do to produce at a low cost if you suffer an overall
loss? If you think about it, the terms *low economic growth* and
stable economic growth are misleading because they indicate that
some growth is still occurring.

During the period of high economic growth, a business
cycle typically consisted of a two- to three-year boom followed
by, at most, a six-month recession. At times the boom lasted
for over three years. With low economic growth, the length of
the recession and boom may be reversed.

It is going to be difficult. The business boom, defined as an
economic growth rate of 6 percent or more, lasts at the most, 6
to 12 months. The growth rate will be lower than that for two
or three years at a time. If things are really bad, the growth rate
may be negative for one or two years.

Don't Be Bound by Conventional Wisdom

Because this is not an age of high economic growth, the production method and philosophy must be different from what they were before.

Ohno: Japanese industry as a whole is used to the notion that what is produced will eventually be sold. Most management is still concerned with quantity.

The *Maxcy-Silberston curve* was frequently used in the auto industry. That theory holds that the cost of producing automobiles drops in direct proportion to the number of automobiles produced. The validity of that curve was proven during the period of high economic growth. Those in the auto industry have been unable to forget this. But now that we have entered a period of low economic growth, it is imperative to stop pursuing the vanishing benefits of mass production as soon as possible.

Production in large lots to realize the benefits of mass production is no longer valid. An example is using the same die press and stamping as many parts as possible during a given period. It must be realized that such practices produce all kinds of waste.

You are saying that it is necessary to shed some elements of conventional wisdom?

Ohno: Yes, you do have to discard some elements of conventional wisdom. First of all, "conventional wisdom" is often something involving no conspicuous advantage or disadvantage. There is a phrase: "It's not dangerous to run a red light if everyone else is doing it." If you compare the advantages with the disadvantages and the former outweigh the latter even slightly, that becomes conventional wisdom. I am not saying that you have to discard all traditional ideas; I am only saying that you must not accept them as limitations. Most people either do not understand this or refuse to believe it. They are afraid of doing the exact opposite of what their predecessors have done and taught them to do.

Taiichi Ohno

Japanese industry, whether as to equipment or plant layout, has always used the United States as a model. This was okay during the period of high economic growth when the economy was growing at a double-digit rate. However, with rapid growth coming to an end and production cutbacks becoming necessary, mass production is no longer profitable. This is only natural.

In 1950 and 1951, right after World War II, we had no idea that automobiles would become as popular as they are now. The practice of reducing the number of car models and using mass production to cut costs had been developed years before in the United States and had permeated American culture. However, in Japan the demand for each model was limited, and manufacturers had to increase the number of models if they were to sell cars in sufficient quantity. The problem we faced was to develop a method for producing a small number of a wide variety of models at a low cost.

After the late 1950s Japan entered a period of high economic growth, and mass production as practiced in the United States provided numerous benefits. However, we remembered that direct imitation of the American type of mass production would be risky. We engaged in high-diversity, small-lot, low-cost production. We believed the Japanese people would be able to do this, that the development of a new production system by the Japanese would enable us to win out over American-style mass production.

Understanding Illusions

You're saying that people should be aware that they may be pursuing illusions.

Ohno: There are many things in this world you can't understand until you try them. With many things, you find that the result is exactly the opposite of what you expected. To convince someone who still believes in an illusion, it is important to have that person try many things to demonstrate to him- or herself that what he or she believes is false.

One thing that I find on almost any production floor is the belief that a job can be done faster if a quantity of parts are done all at once. When you tell someone to produce a whole product at a time, people frequently say that this is inefficient, that repeatedly performing only one step at a time improves efficiency and productivity.

At one company, I saw a worker inspecting the final products. She would lay them on a table and inspect one after another. When she had finished a number of them she would stop inspecting and pack them. I told her that the job would be easier and more efficient if she would inspect and pack one item at a time. She insisted, however, that her method was better. I finally convinced her to inspect one item at a time for one day. She found that the new method was easier and that she could inspect 5,000 items a day without overtime, which was impossible under the previous method. The woman was convinced when she tried the new method. There must be numerous such examples on any production floor.

I had a similar experience at Toyota Jiko. I saw a young worker manually drilling a hole in a rod. I told him that he could use automatic feeding for that process. He told me that if automatic feeding was used, the drill tip would become blunt and break off or degrade the hole's dimensional accuracy. I asked him how long it took him to drill a hole. He told me he could do it in 30 seconds per rod. I replied to him: "That means you can drill two rods per minute." He said: "Yes." I said: "That means 120 rods per hour." He was reluctant to answer. I continued: "If it takes 30 seconds to drill a rod, that means you could drill 120 rods per hour." The worker had been boasting that he could drill 80 rods in seven hours. I asked him why it took him seven hours to drill 80 rods when it should have taken him only 40 minutes. He had no answer.

We knew that it took 40 seconds to drill a hole using automatic feeding and that the same job took 30 seconds when manual feeding was used. This created the illusion that manual feeding was faster. When holes were drilled rapidly one after another, the drill tip became overheated and blunt after the drilling of about three rods. The worker would then take the drill to a grinder and re-grind the bit. He would then drill some three more rods and again return to the grinder. He assumed that grinding the drill bit was part of his work. When the rods were drilled using automatic feeding at a proper cutting rate, it took 40 seconds to drill a hole. After the hole was drilled, the next four minutes and 20 seconds were used to cool the bit. This allowed the next rod to be drilled at the normal drill bit temperature. When the bit became hot, cutting oil was poured on the blade. After four minutes or so of this, the bit's temperature would drop to that of the cutting oil. Using this procedure it was possible to drill 30 to 50 rods without re-grinding the bit.

What I am saying is that even though manual drilling allowed only three or four rods to be drilled in ten minutes, the worker believed that it took only 30 seconds and that he was faster than a machine. A worker may believe that he or she is a skillful, hard worker, but the truth may be the opposite. I feel that inefficient job practices are tolerated on many production floors.

The Dangers of Mathematical Calculation

It must take courage to tell individuals that they are mistaken, that they believe in an illusion and must change their ways.

Ohno: In many companies everyone from top management to middle management, maybe even down to production-floor workers, believes that their present way is the best, or at least the most reasonable. They are a bunch of self-deluders. They cannot get away from the "common-sense" way of doing their job. Every company has a labor union. Labor unions are formed by people. They also believe in illusions and resist attempts to change existing ways. I believe that a company cannot continue to survive unless a revolution of consciousness takes place, involving everyone from top management to the ordinary workers and even the labor unions.

It is very difficult on a production floor to eliminate the belief that mass production is more efficient and cheaper than producing items one at a time. This is especially true when someone adept at numbers comes along and starts talking about cost. It is so easy to believe in the illusion that with a press, for example, it is much cheaper to stamp 10,000 pieces using the same setup than 1,000 pieces. When this illusion is supported by numbers, people then believe that the illusion is the truth.

It is so easy mathematically to "prove" that it is inefficient, for example, not to stamp for at least two hours if the setup takes one hour: that producing more will reduce cost regardless of whether the setup takes ten minutes or an hour: or that the advantages of reducing the set-up time to ten minutes are lost if the lot size is also reduced at the same time. These mathematical calculations are based on a completely different set of assumptions. It is useless to respond to them directly. The only thing we can say is: "Yes, that's true as far as it goes."

You're saying that the belief that mass production reduces costs and that mass sales increase profits — which may be corroborated by mathematical calculations — can nevertheless be wrong under certain circumstances.

Ohno: We always say to produce as much as can be sold and no more than that. When this is seen from a mathematical approach, people end up saying: "What's wrong with you? Producing 20 instead of 10 reduces costs." Ignoring the amount that can be sold and concentrating only on the cost-reducing potential is a mistake frequently made by believers in mathematical calculation.

Limited, Not Leaner, Management

Now that we have entered a period of low economic growth, many companies are stressing "leaner" management. You use the phrase "limited" management, rather than leaner management.

Ohno: The idea is to produce only what can be sold and no more. The idea is to *limit*, not necessarily to *reduce*, the quantity. The important thing is to keep production costs low while limiting the production level. It is meaningless to say that producing 15,000 units will reduce production costs when you can only sell 10,000 units. If they sell, the company will make a profit, but if they don't, the company will suffer a loss.

Of course, it is possible that producing 15,000 units instead of 10,000 will reduce costs. But if only 10,000 units are sold and the remaining 5,000 units gather dust sitting in a warehouse, is that a profit? If only 10,000 units can be sold, the idea is to produce 10,000 at the lowest possible cost. Producing 10,000 may mean a higher per-unit cost than producing 15,000, but the essence of limited management and limited production is to produce what can be sold at the lowest possible cost.

It is generally accepted that mass production reduces costs and that small-lot production is expensive. This is a commonly held view. However, I have visited many companies and plants, and, from my experience, it is very rare that increased production actually reduces costs. In most cases increased production means increased costs.

The reason is that the production capability of any production floor is pretty much determined in advance. For example, if a press can turn out 1,000 stampings per hour, does it reduce the overall cost to try to run it at a rate of 1,200 stampings per hour?

Because you can't buy a second press immediately, you decide to work overtime to produce 20 percent more. Many companies have to pay 30 or 40 percent more in wages for overtime. So if you work overtime and produce 12,000 items, the real cost has risen because of the increased labor costs. Because labor unions oppose overtime, you decide to buy a second press. Even though you've bought the second unit, the amount of work doesn't increase quickly. This means that the utilization rate of the second unit remains low for some time. This makes the equipment expensive. For this and other reasons, it is possible for increased production to increase costs, not reduce them, until some threshold value is reached.

You mustn't forget either that costs can go down as you produce less. For example, if the set-up time for a press is reduced from one hour to ten minutes, you spend ten minutes setting up the press for stamping part A. You then spend ten minutes actually stamping part A, producing several dozens of the part. You then spend another ten minutes setting up the press for stamping part B and ten more minutes actually stamping it. Lastly, you spend ten minutes setting up the press for stamping part C and again, ten minutes stamping part C, a large-lot production item. This means that during the set-up time saved, you have produced about 50 small-lot items. This meant that these items were produced without cost.

An interesting fact is that consumers also believe mass production reduces costs and small-lot production increases them. Manufacturers take advantage of this and charge more when you order in small quantities.

Ohno: Yes. Because there is an accepted view that mass production reduces costs and that small-lot production increases them, manufacturers can charge more for small-lot production items. There is an opportunity for manufacturers to make lots of money so long as the general public believes that high-diversity, small-lot production is expensive. As long as society believes in an illusion — and there are many companies operating under that illusion — smart companies that engage in high-diversity, small-lot production can make lots of money.

When you start calculating the unit production cost for each item and start sorting items into profitable and unprofitable ones, you end up saying that small-lot production is very expensive. You may end up not producing the most "profitable" item because calculations show that it isn't profitable. It is also possible to mass produce and sell what is actually not a profitable item. I think there are many such examples.

Many people believe that the Toyota production system is a method for reducing inventory or eliminating inventory altogether.

Ohno: That's not right. I've said this so many times, but people don't seem to understand. The Toyota production system is a philosophy of changing the production and management flows. One time when I visited a company, the company official told me proudly: "We have reduced the inventory. We have achieved limited management." In checking, I found they had simply reduced the amount of raw materials. I asked them: "Aren't you going to have problems with production now that you have reduced the stockpile of raw materials?" He said no. I noticed in the factory that all the raw materials had been converted into work-in-process. This is not reducing inventory. Raw materials and raw ingredients are not counted as part of inventory, but work-in-process is.

Agricultural People Love Inventory

Ohno: Present-day Japanese are the descendants of an agricultural race. We have a heritage as an agricultural people. An agricultural race lives at one location and cultivates food on nearby farms. The crop yield varies widely with weather and other natural phenomena. A typhoon or a dry spell can wipe out the harvest. Lying deep within our hearts is the notion that we must harvest and store as much as we can, when we can. We have retained a similar attitude even in our plants and factories that are pretty much unaffected by weather and such factors. It is hard for us to shed the belief that it is best to produce as much as we can, when we can, in order to guard against an equipment breakdown or employee absenteeism.

With farming, it is necessary to harvest and store as much rice as you can to guard against a famine. The idea is to store as much as possible, to increase the inventory. Companies do the same thing — they try to produce and hoard. This requires them to build warehouses. Once you start storing inventory in warehouses, you need computers and people to manage the inventory. Once a warehouse building project is started, people build the warehouses a little larger than absolutely necessary. People don't realize that this thinking gets you deeper and deeper into a quagmire.

Of course, just reducing inventory reduces the company's interest payments. When inventory is reduced by, say, ¥100 million, most people who deal with numbers think that the benefit is only the reduction of several million yen in interest payments. It's actually not that simple. Have you heard the proverb: "Abundant harvest, falling prices"? A large rice harvest depresses the price of rice. Even with fishing, if the catch is large enough, the fishermen virtually don't care if you take a fish without paying. A bumper crop or a bumper catch reduces the price. When the crop or catch is limited, people are willing to pay more for what is in short supply. This raises the price. It has always been important in business to know that too big a supply is not good. The problem is not related only to interest payments.

Inventory means that funds are tied up. There is a saying, "Money begets money." Funds must be actively used.

The advantages of small-lot or single-unit production include shortened delivery times.

Ohno: Most manufacturers mass-produce. They think that this reduces the unit cost — but that is a mistake. They need one completed unit in order to sell. However, two or three days are spent producing parts while not a single completed unit is made. On the fourth day the end products emerge in mass quantity.

You have to use single-unit production. You can't shorten the delivery period as long as you produce in parts. It is important to produce in units of one. Most people understand this theoretically. But they forget it when they get to the production floor. They believe that producing one item at a time is too expensive.

For example, if you have to stamp 10,000 sheets each of A and B and spot-weld the two, the conventional approach is to stamp 10,000 sheets of A and then 10,000 sheets of B. The idea is that it is less costly to mass-stamp one part at a time. However, while you are stamping 10,000 sheets of A, not a single sheet of B is produced. This means that the workers down the line cannot do any welding. Suppose it takes one second to stamp A, one second to stamp B, and one second to spot-weld the two. This makes a total of three seconds. If you were to stamp 10,000 sheets of A first, the workers down the line would have to wait 10,000 seconds before they could do anything. Not a single completed unit is produced during that time.

Actually, at least one completed unit should be produced every four seconds: one second to stamp A, one second to stamp B, one second to align the two, and one second to spot-weld the two. If you don't think it is strange that for more than 10,000 seconds nothing is produced, something's wrong with you. How long does it take for an order to be delivered? They say it takes one month to produce 10,000. However, the customer actually needs 100 pieces every day, not the entire order at once. If 10,000 pieces arrive at once, the customer will be saddled with an inventory. It is better for the manufacturer to produce and deliver 100 pieces every day. This will reduce the customer's inventory as well.

Profitable Companies Cannot Do It

We are told that the basic philosophy of the Toyota production system is the total elimination of waste. Some companies reject the Toyota production system.

Ohno: Companies that are making even a modest profit never use the Toyota production system. They can't. On the other hand, there are nearly bankrupt companies that implement the Toyota production system to the fullest, knowing that they won't lose much even if it fails, and that do manage to turn the company around in two or three months. This is the advantage of a defiant attitude. There are many examples of the Toyota production system working well in downstream processing companies such as garment manufacturers. But many companies that produce the fabric used in making the clothing (the upstream processing companies) reject the Toyota production system. The reason is that the textile industry has had a glorious past. During the Taisho (1912-1925) and the early Showa (1926-present) eras, the textile industry boomed. The industry also prospered during the ten-year period after World War II. Many people in the industry still think the traditional method is good. Top management cannot make any drastic changes. One commonly hears: "This is the way our competitors do it. This is the way the industry is." Even if the industry may be in a recession, there are ways to survive it.

Companies that are doing fairly well become picky. If a company is willing to adopt only what seems appealing, it might as well not adopt any of it. Companies make a big mistake in implementing the Toyota production system thinking that it is just a production method. The Toyota production method won't work unless it is used as an overall management system. The Toyota production system is not something that can be used only on the production floors. The belief that it is only a production method is fundamentally wrong.

A former subordinate of mine at Toyota now teaches the Toyota production system at NPS. NPS accepts only one company from each industry. It is not open to everyone. It is difficult to implement the Toyota production system without good instructors or on your own. It cannot be learned from a book. Implementing book knowledge is difficult because much of the method runs counter to conventional wisdom. But timely guidance from a good instructor can produce a lot of progress.

One of the basic tenets of the Toyota production system is the just-in-time philosophy. This means that the parts necessary for assembling a car arrive at the assembly line just when the parts are needed in the quantity necessary. This is an ideal state in terms of production management. However, automobiles are made up of thousands of parts. It is extremely difficult to plan the production processes so that all parts arrive just in time.

Production plans must be changed continuously due to mistaken forecasting, clerical errors, equipment failures, defects, employee absences, and so forth. Unless a company has the ability to cope with changes in the production plan, it is bound to face shortages of parts that could lead to a stoppage of the assembly line and create production turmoil.

If a company adheres to a production scheme without developing contingency plans, problems such as over- or underproduction of parts and a rapid rise in an inventory of unneeded parts can occur. This reduces production efficiency and the efficiency of the company.

Worse, it becomes difficult to distinguish the abnormal from the normal on a production line. This can lead to anomalies and uncorrected overproduction.

Succeeding with Just-In-Time
Requires a Totally Restructured System

In traditional manufacturing systems, a production plan is drawn up in the same order as the sequence of processes the materials will go through as they are assembled into a product. In the Toyota production system, however, the required number of parts is fed into the appropriate process as the parts are needed. In implementing just-in-time, it is better not to reveal the production plans for different processes or to have a plan for a prior process to pass along parts to later processes. This seems to turn the usual production plan system on its head.

Ohno: In ordinary companies, the information as to "what, when, and how many" is provided by the planning department to the production floors using forms such as the work-in-process planning sheet, delivery planning sheet, production instruction sheet, delivery instruction sheet, and so on. With this method, the interpretation of "when" is left up to the recipient. It is okay as long as the parts arrive on time; being too early is not considered a problem. But handling parts produced too early takes the time of workers. The importance of the just-in-time approach is in the word *just*; it does no good to be simply *on time*.

A tool can be harmful if it is used in the wrong way. Kanban, which are the tools for operating the Toyota production method, can produce problems if used improperly.

One of the rules for the use of kanban is for the later processes to come to the earlier processes to pick up the necessary parts (a "pull" system). This rule is contrary to conventional wisdom and cannot be implemented simply by understanding it. The company's top management must revolutionize the consciousness of the workers so as to turn around the flow of production, transportation, and delivery from what they formerly were (a "push" system). Many resist this. Implementing the Toyota production system requires courage.

This is because a pull system — the act of later processes going to the earlier processes to retrieve only what is needed, when it is needed — can shake the entire foundation of the business and company if improperly implemented. A pull system leads to the abolishment of the daily planning sheets that workers are so familiar with. There is considerable resistance among production workers when they are not told in advance what to produce. In addition, the subassembly lines try to produce only what is actually retrieved by the later processes, the problem of setup changes arises on all production lines except dedicated lines. There is also a need to minimize the lot size.

The greatest problem occurs when the later process habitually picks up the same item en masse, leaving the earlier process facing a parts shortage. A system such as this leads the earlier processes to build up an inventory of many parts to avoid a parts shortage. Carried to its extreme, this system can cause a factory to become flooded with inventory. Hence, achieving a system whereby later processes pick up what is needed from the earlier processes requires changing the operation of the earlier processes as well as that of the later processes.

Implementing the Toyota production system means nothing less than the total recasting of the existing production system. Therefore, those who decide to implement the Toyota production system must be fully committed. If you try to adopt only the "good parts," you'll fail.

The Dangers of Computers and Robots

You say that computers and robots should not be installed indiscriminately. Why?

Ohno: We are not opposed to computers and robots. The performance of computers and robots is continuously improving. However, one must always question the practice of installing computers and robots without first considering the drop in costs that they are intended to provide. Robots and numerical control equipment are selling well in Japan, but the important thing is the extent to which they reduce costs. If this were an age in which everything produced could be sold, the use of robots would probably always reduce costs. There is no denying that robots reduce the number of processes. If you calculate production costs by the number of processes, robots do produce at a very low cost.

The strongest justification for installing robots is cost reduction. A second justification, even in the absence of cost reduction, is eliminating inhuman tasks. It is wrong, however, to install a robot and start producing unnecessary goods just to keep the robot busy. This only increases inventory.

Under the Toyota production system, it is important to achieve *autonomation* rather than *automation*. It is important to operate automatically, not just to automate.

There are many items of equipment that run automatically once you flick a switch. But because modern equipment runs fast, a small abnormality can result in dozens, even hundreds, of defective goods. This can also happen with robots.

Autonomated operation is different from simply operating *unattended*. Producing defects is not constructive work. With autonomation, the equipment must stop itself when a defect is produced. It is necessary to build into the machine a system for distinguishing good parts from bad parts to prevent production of defective goods.

The notion of *stopping* is intrinsic to the concept of autonomation. One definition of autonomated equipment is a machine that can be automatically stopped. Proper operation includes automatic stopping. At Toyota's plants, all equipment, old and new, is equipped with automatic stopping devices embodying such methods as the *prescribed-position stopping method*, the *full work system*, or the *mistake-proof system*. The equipment is endowed with human perception, sometimes referred to as "automation with a human touch."

Autonomation is not just unattended operation — it alters the management method significantly. It allows a machine to be operated unattended as long as it runs properly. A human worker becomes necessary only when the machine stops due to some abnormality. This allows one worker to handle a number of machines at one time, reducing the number of processes, and increasing the production efficiency dramatically.

It does not apply only to the automobile industry but to the fashion industry as well. Conventional wisdom held that sewing machines had to be operated sitting down. It is a departure from conventional wisdom to operate them standing up. In the textile industry today, however, operating sewing machines while standing is becoming the norm. Speed is not the only goal. It is important to achieve autonomation so that sewing machines can run unattended. If the sewing machine is designed to stop when a problem develops, then a single worker can handle not one but five or six machines.

At Aisin Kikai, a Toyota group company in the textile industry that is promoting the Toyota production system, sewing machines are produced at half their previous cost. The company wanted each worker to handle more than three machines, so they needed a cost reduction of more than 33 percent. The company sells sewing machines at a lower cost, along with know-how. They are now conducting their business in a manner appropriate to the new age.

A Foreman Should Monitor the Work, Not the Worker

Rationalization is a by-word on the production floors of many companies. However, rationalization is not pushed in the offices of the same companies. How can office work be rationalized?

Ohno: Office work and production are the same. *On-site-ism* [a literal translation of the original Japanese, which is *genba shugi*] means stressing the importance of the actual site, which can even be an office. It is fairly easy to visualize what happens on a production floor. This is not the case in company offices. If a worker appears to be working diligently, it is very difficult for a manager to tell whether he or she is doing something that should be done now. In office departments, department managers do not consider themselves "foremen" nor are they familiar with all of the clerical tasks. They consider themselves "managers," but what is actually needed is a foreman — someone who is able to teach.

A manager can get by on knowledge alone. A foreman, however, needs knowledge and must also be able to perform and demonstrate the task at hand in order to serve as an example. Evaluating job results is also a problem. In Japan, foremen traditionally tend to monitor how a worker is working, not the job being done. This mistake is made on production floors and in company offices. Whereas foremen should actually supervise job performance, they instead supervise the worker methods.

In the world of professional baseball, the manager is important. If a manager is incompetent, the team will suffer. It is also true that great players don't necessarily make great managers. A manager must know each player well — from his personality to his baseball ability — in order to function properly as a manager. White-collar workers on the promotion ladder move up from one job to another. They do not experience the essence of the workplace. They think only of moving up to the next rung after a certain number of years.

Managers and foremen generally make no effort to outper-form their predecessors. They are bureaucrats. They want to stay out of trouble so that they can be promoted. This may be the problem.

Companies that have not succeeded in revolutionizing their CEOs' thinking will face problems.

Ohno: With companies whose ordinary profit is less than their operating profit, I wonder for whom the workers are working. If workers have to work just so that the company can make interest payments to the banks, the company president should be embarrassed.

One hundred million yen ($800,000) is not much these days. Until now, company presidents did not mind borrowing ¥1 billion or ¥10 billion from a bank, treating 20 percent or so of the loan as profit, and paying back several percent as interest to the bank. This was okay during the late 1950s and the early 1960s, but now it is very hard to achieve a 20 percent return on an investment. There just is no business that profitable.

But company owners who believe in the old ways hesitate to repay their loans. Instead, they want to use all available funds to expand their business for more profit. I tell them: "Pay your debts. Use your head, not your money, to repay your loans." If there are available funds after paying back the loans, I don't mind them expanding the business. Even if the business does not grow, the only thing lost — as long as the sought-for ex-pansion was financed with internal funds and the company has not been saddled with interest payments — is the oppor-tunity to have used the funds more wisely.

PART FOUR

Implementing NPS

CHAPTER FOURTEEN

Ending the Myth of Mass Production

WHAT DOES NPS tell its members to do in order to invigorate and revive a slumping company? NPS's basic philosophy is to produce one item at a time, just in time, using one setup, with the later processes determining the output of the prior processes. The philosophy is to produce not in large lots but in the smallest lot sizes, if possible in lots of one item or one piece at a time. Kinoshita says: "Because one is the smallest unit, producing one item at a time is the ideal. Members should think hard to see what can be done to get as close as possible to the ideal."

Producing in a lot size of one is easier said than done, especially for those who have been lifelong practitioners of mass production. An understandable criticism is that producing in a lot size of one is too laborious and inefficient.

Low-diversity, large-lot production is theoretically more efficient and cheaper than high-diversity, small-lot production. Conventional wisdom says that producing one item at a time is time consuming, inefficient, and expensive. NPS says this is false.

According to Suzumura: "Small-lot and single-piece production can indeed be inefficient. Mass production is cheaper, but only under certain conditions. One condition is that all the products can be sold. What are you going to do if you can't sell everything you manufacture?"

It is no longer true that mass production will automatically make a company more competitive. In fact, many companies are actually strangling themselves by overproduction. During the period of high economic growth in Japan, companies suffering from overproduction and excessive inventory were rescued by periodic buying sprees on the part of the consumers.

However, it is generally accepted that the age of high economic growth in Japan has been replaced by an age of low, stable growth. It is not only the economic cycles that make massive sales of goods unlikely. Manufacturers can no longer rely on consumer buying sprees; consumer tastes and needs are becoming diversified. Also, consider the speed with which new technology is developed. Today's innovation becomes obsolete and is cast aside in only a matter of months.

NPS refers the situation in which demand outstrips supply as Pattern A. When supply exceeds demand, this is Pattern B. Manufacturers continue to believe in the myth of mass production and its resultant cost reduction even in the age of low, stable growth. They refuse to acknowledge that their belief was applicable only in the age of Pattern A, and that the old business philosophy is now dead.

Suzumura says:

> In the age of Pattern B, it is necessary to think of everything in terms of one. The quantity "ten" should not be thought of as one indivisible unit but as equal to "one times ten." You repeat one, ten times, to get ten. You repeat one, a hundred times, to get one hundred. The shortest path to surviving in the age of Pattern B is to think of a best method for producing one and repeating the method as many times as necessary.

NPS says that there is a fundamental difference between one (singular) and two (plural). One multiplied by itself is one, no matter how many times you do the multiplication. However, two multiplied by two increases as you repeat the operation. Two times one is two, but two times two is four. This is the difference between one and any other number. NPS says that there is no intrinsic difference between producing two, five, or ten at a time. What they have in common is that they are not producing one at a time. NPS says that the starting point is to produce in units of one and to dispel such an ambiguous notion as a high-diversity, small-lot production.

NPS does not accept high-diversity, small-lot production as a production goal. Instead it asks: "What is a 'small lot'? The best thing is to produce not in small lots but in units of 'one.' Work hard to make this possible."

A trend seen among both wholesalers and retailers is to reduce inventory. This trend will make it necessary for manufacturers to produce a large diversity of goods in small-lot sizes with minimum lead time. A typical example is of subcontractors delivering parts to Pattern B auto manufacturers such as Toyota. Such auto manufacturers do not carry inventory. Instead, they tell their subcontractors to produce a part when it is needed, only in the amount necessary. This practice is spreading to manufacturers in other industries.

Spreading Just-In-Time to the Distribution Industry

The just-in-time method is spreading to the distribution industry as well. Supermarkets exploded in popularity during Japan's period of high economic growth. This was made possible by volume purchases and volume sales, which reduced purchase and resale costs. However, for the consumers this is the age of abundance and surplus. Regardless of how hard the volume discount stores try to entice customers into buying, customers buy only what they need. This is not an age when stores can stack piles of merchandise, discount their price, and expect the customers to buy them. However, many supermarkets are still the embodiment of excess, waste, and unevenness [these are expressed in Japanese as *muri*, *muda*, and *mura*, or the "three Ms"].

Times are changing, and the distribution industry is searching for new business practices. Masatoshi Ito, president of Ito-Yokado, says:

> We must discard all concepts developed during the "age of consumption." We must search for the management method and the corporate structure that fits the "age of limited consumption" in order for us to survive the competition. How can we adapt quickly to the changing needs of the consumers? Is it possible to maintain our profit level when fewer goods are being sold?

Taiichi Ohno says: "Ito-Yokado, the supermarket chain, was the first company in the distribution industry to come to us to study the Toyota production system." In fact, Ito-Yokado was the first in the distribution industry to study the Toyota production system and implement a policy of purchasing only what is necessary, when necessary, and only in the amount necessary. Ito-Yokado is now using a Point of Sale (POS) management system in order to further enhance its just-in-time policy.

Of course, Ito-Yokado is not the only company with a policy of eliminating excess, waste, and unevenness. Many companies in the distribution industry, notably Daiei, Nichii, and Marui, have the same policy.

The trend among supermarkets, department stores, and even ordinary retailers is to stop carrying inventory and require their suppliers to deliver only enough products to replace what has been sold.

The suppliers will no longer be able to say: "We'll deliver it in a month," or "We can't deliver it any sooner than a week from now." The suppliers will lose their customers to their competitors unless they can promptly produce and deliver what is ordered.

The survival of all companies in the future depends on whether they can quickly respond to customer orders. Of course, low prices are important, but the company must also be competitive in terms of delivery deadline and quality even for small-lot orders. These very difficult demands must be met for a company to survive. Kinoshita says:

> The NPS method allows the required goods to be produced at the required time in the required quantity. If the customer wants it now, you produce it and deliver it now. Other companies won't be able do this, so we shall be very competitive. I expect the gap between us and other companies to continue to widen.

This is understandable. Those who place an order want the order to be filled today or tomorrow. If it takes a week or a month to fill the order, the customer will turn to a company that can produce the order faster.

Restricting Production Quantity to Actual Demand

Besides producing only one at a time, another NPS tenet is to limit production quantity to actual demand. A conventional production practice is for the earlier processes to dictate the flow of parts to the later processes. As an example, consider the production of a TV set. The raw materials are processed into parts, the parts are assembled, and the cathode-ray tube is installed. The assembled parts are finally placed in a cabinet.

A problem with this procedure of letting the earlier processes dictate the downstream flow of goods is that the earlier processes are unaware of what is happening in the later processes. The result is that the earlier processes in the manufacture of the parts allow only for their own circumstances and make no allowance for conditions further down the line. Moreover, to avoid a parts shortage in the later processes, the earlier processes tend to overproduce and keep an inventory of parts in order to avoid a parts shortage. This overproduction is a major cause of a drop in the productivity and efficiency of a company.

Taiichi Ohno thought of reversing the production flow. Ohno decided that it would be better to let the later processes go to the prior processes and get the needed parts only when necessary and only in the amount necessary. This would allow the earlier processes to manufacture only what is actually used by the subsequent processes. This would prevent overproduction by the earlier processes while avoiding a parts shortage, and eventually, reducing the number of semifinished and defective goods.

To implement the practice described above, the production plan is shown to the final assembly line, which is instructed to retrieve only the parts that are necessary from the earlier processes, only when the parts are necessary, and only in the amount necessary. This limits the output of the earlier processes to the amount actually required by the later processes. This process of limiting prior production to actual demand is carried further upward until it reaches the raw materials procurement department.

Diversifying by Moving Upstream

World, an apparel manufacturer and NPS member, reportedly considered purchasing Descente, another apparel manufacturer, when Descente was facing serious financial difficulties due to massive losses. When a representative of World discussed this matter with Kinoshita, the latter reportedly said: "Don't do such a petty thing. It is better for companies to be strong vertically than to be wide horizontally. If you have the money to buy Descente, buy a dye or fabric manufacturer. Move up."

Kinoshita's reasoning was as follows. In this age of slow economic growth, companies are diversifying to maintain an acceptable profit level. Companies realize that their growth potential is limited if they stick only to their principal line of business. Another motive for diversifying is to absorb the surplus labor created by greater efficiency.

Broadly speaking, there are three paths to business diversification. One is to enter a field totally different from one's principal line of business. The idea of this is to strengthen the company by establishing a new business pillar. The second is to enter a field peripherally related to one's principal business. Here the idea is to increase your present strength. The third path is to diversify by moving downstream. An example is a fabric manufacturer expanding into the apparel business.

Kinoshita holds that companies should not diversify recklessly. He doubts that a company not doing well in its principal business can succeed in a new venture.

There are numerous examples of companies diversifying as a stepping stone to the future or to create the next business pillar. But how many of these diversifications succeed? Of course, there are companies that add depth to their business by an unexpected success in a new field. There are also many companies for which a new business becomes the principal business.

However, for some companies a careless diversification creates serious business problems that adversely affect even their principal business. It must be realized that diversification does not guarantee profits. How can a company without knowledge of the production basics turn to manufacturing a different item using its same old philosophy and succeed in creating high-quality goods at low cost? The grass may be greener on the other side of the fence, but it may not stay greener just because you move there. You have to understand what made the grass greener.

Rapid change is taking place in every facet of our lives, technology included. A company may be the first to enter a new field, but competitors will immediately jump in if it is profitable. Without a decisive advantage such as a patent right, there is nothing to guarantee that the first entrant into a field will not be overtaken by a later one. This has happened many times.

For these reasons, Kinoshita repeatedly warns NPS member companies never to diversify or start new product development without careful reflection. He also instructs member companies promptly to dismantle departments created by diversification and to concentrate instead on their main business if the diversification does not appear to be working out.

When consulted about World's purchase of Descente, Kinoshita immediately advised against it. He advised instead to move upstream if the funds are there. Many companies move downstream, the reason being a downstream move promises greater value addition, hence higher profitability.

However, any profitable business faces tremendous competition. If World instead creates an integrated production system by purchasing a dye manufacturer and a fabric manufacturer, it will become much more competitive — probably the strongest in the industry.

The number of supermarkets having their own production facilities is very small. Even among co-ops, the Kobe Nada Co-op in Kansai is probably the only one with a production department, albeit a limited one. However, producing your own merchandise provides a greater profit margin than purchasing from the outside. Kinoshita says: "We like manufacturing industries. NPS will provide guidance only to those in the manufacturing sector." However, if NPS decides to serve companies in the distribution industry, it will probably advise them to develop their own manufacturing capabilities. This is in line with NPS's philosophy of moving upstream.

Most managements move downstream when diversifying. NPS, however, teaches companies to cast aside some aspects of conventional wisdom, to believe what many do not believe. NPS says that by moving upstream hidden treasures are found — yet another example of NPS going contrary to conventional wisdom.

Not a Poor Imitation of the Kanban Method

The NPS philosophy is to limit production quantity to actual demand. The purpose is to eliminate all waste and inventory, which are physical and financial burdens on a business. If the just-in-time system is perfected, that is, if the production quantity is limited to actual demand so that each process receives from an earlier process only what is needed, when needed, and in the amount needed, inventory will become unnecessary.

However, making sure that parts actually arrive just-in-time is difficult because the earlier processes do not know which parts and how many of them are needed for the subsequent processes. The kanban (work-order sheet) is used as a tool and method for linking the different processes so that demand information is readily available.

NPS also uses kanban, which some say means that the NPS production method is no different from Toyota's production system or kanban method.

It is true that the NPS production method is derived from both the kanban and the Toyota production system. However, the mere fact that kanban are used does not mean that the NPS production method is the kanban method. Kanban are only a means, a tool, and tools can be used in many ways. For example, there are many different schools of Japanese swordsmanship (*shindoryu, shininryu, ittoryu, nitoryu* à la Musashi

Miyamoto, etc.), even though they all use the same weapon.

When Taiichi Ohno and Kikuo Suzumura were at Toyota developing the Toyota production system, they were concerned only with production and indeed, the Toyota production method was a production method. Organizational constraints prevented it from being used for purposes other than production. NPS, however, is not concerned solely with production. To say that the NPS method is the kanban method — just because pieces of paper are used to indicate the flow of goods between processes — is a gross misrepresentation of the whole picture.

CHAPTER FIFTEEN

Motivating the Workers on the Production Floor

THE BASIC philosophy of the NPS Research Association is:

1. To seek a production technology that uses a minimum amount of equipment and labor to produce defect-free goods in the shortest possible time with the least amount of unfinished goods left over; and
2. To regard as waste any element that does not contribute to meeting the quality, price, or delivery deadline required by the customer, and to strive to eliminate all waste through concerted efforts by the administration, R & D, production, distribution, management, and all other departments of the company.

A document entitled *The Basic Doctrine of the NPS Research Association* states that:

1. A company's employees spend the major portion of their lives at the company. As such, the company must provide true work to the workers and must learn what true work really is.
2. Because Japan does not have any natural resources, the nation's survival depends on its processing technology. Improving production technology is imperative.

3. People are mortal, but a company must live on and
   grow forever. To make this possible, each company
   must develop a philosophy to be passed on forever
   to posterity.

NPS's beliefs and philosophy are not unique or original. We
have all heard such before. A difference may be that most companies preach but do not practice their beliefs. NPS practices
what it preaches.

Becoming a Believer

Noboru Kawasaki says: "A company that has even a shred
of doubt about NPS will not succeed. You must believe in it.
NPS is like the Lotus Sutra [a Buddhist text that teaches universal salvation]." If you believe in it, you'll be saved. The
quickest path to success is to imbue the entire company with
the NPS philosophy.

This is why NPS first determines whether the company
president can become an all-out believer in NPS, from head to
toe. If the president is noncommittal, the board of directors
cannot be persuaded. And without a solid commitment on the
part of the top management, the employees won't become
wholehearted believers in NPS either.

NPS therefore starts by educating and "brainwashing" the
company president. As Kinoshita has said, NPS is looking for
companies that are so committed to passing the NPS philosophy along to posterity that they are willing even to include
it in their articles of incorporation. The importance of starting
the training with the company president is obvious. Because
most presidents are already committed to NPS when their
company seeks membership, it does not take long for the president to understand and internalize the NPS philosophy.
Moreover, even if some things may not be well understood,
the important thing is to believe wholeheartedly in what the

Director or the Chairman of the Implementation Committee says. The specific details can be left to the instructors.

This requirement of total commitment to NPS is probably what makes NPS appear like a cult or religion to outsiders. However, what NPS is saying is to practice it before doubting it. Practicing it will make you a believer. Of course, this is hard for some people to do, and some companies will not become members of NPS. In five or ten years, the management style of those who joined versus those who did not will become as different as night and day.

It is interesting to note that company presidents who are the boss at their own companies become as obedient as kindergarten or grade-school pupils when facing the Director of NPS or a member of the Implementation Committee. Every January the president and three select executives of each member company attend a general convention of NPS. Though the meeting is held in January, there is no festive New Year's mood in evidence.

At the convention, the company presidents stand up one by one to report and reflect on the current state of their companies. If a member company has failed to meet its goals, the audience may demand an explanation or openly criticize the president for lack of hard work, or even suggest that the company withdraw from NPS. Of course, no president has resigned because of such criticisms. The presidents realize that the criticism makes them better managers.

Those That Quit and Those That Rejoice

Since even the company presidents are not spared open criticism, it is easy to imagine that the NPS instructors do not mince words when giving instruction on the production floors. For example, in one of his visits to the Kambara Plant of Nippon Light Metal, Suzumura, with his body shaking and his face flushed with anger, yelled at the plant manager and other plant executives for not getting rid of the piles of work-in-process as he had told them to do on an earlier visit. Suzumura kicked and scattered a pile of half-finished goods, then took off his helmet and slammed it on the floor. The plant manager and the others who witnessed this tirade turned pale. Suzumura stood firm, motionless.

Suzumura was not acting; he was truly angry. Even though this was not his own company, he was so committed to improving it that he could not tolerate people who did less than their best.

These days, many company presidents are so afraid of hurting workers' feelings that they don't say what ought to be said. They let somebody else do the criticizing. The NPS people do not shilly-shally. If the NPS instructors were the compromising sort, they would not be asked to help in the first place. When a company president comes to NPS, bows his head, and asks for NPS's help, and NPS grants the request, NPS becomes totally committed to helping the company.

If those on the production floor refuse to heed what the NPS instructor says, NPS will pull out its instructor, stop advising the production-floor leaders, and terminate its involvement. This has happened rather frequently in the past. When it does happen, the floor leaders often resign from the company.

Suzumura says: "Using NPS can result in workers quitting the company. Don't follow the quitters. Instead, clasp your hands, bow your head, and say: 'This cuts costs by many hundreds of thousands of dollars.'"

NPS may sound cruel. Some may say that it has no compassion in showing up one day, turning everything upside down, and then disregarding people who quit as a result. Some say that the admonition to treat people with respect found in NPS's basic doctrine is not reflected in their behavior.

It is interesting to note that those who quit are the foremen and others in management who persist in sticking to the old methods and refusing to change their ways. This is understandable. Those who have spent long comfortable years as managers and foremen, never having to show any creativity, have nowhere to turn when told that they are on the wrong track. They have no way of venting their anger when the methods they have spent their careers developing are discredited and cast aside.

But how do their subordinates feel? Some subordinates may quit their jobs out of loyalty to their superiors. However, most of them will welcome the new situation because they know that the new system will improve their workplace. NPS is resisted only by those who try to cling to their outdated positions and nurse their wounded pride.

NPS is a threat to those whose past practices are discredited. It is not a threat to those who look to the future. For them, NPS is a wonderful thing that promises better profitability for the company and job security.

Kinoshita, Suzumura, and the NPS instructors do not wear scowls on their faces from morning to night. They are actually friendly and warm, and enjoy joking and making people laugh. As the NPS philosophy takes root in the workplace, its atmosphere becomes brighter than ever before. The workers know that the workplace belongs to them and that the NPS movement allows people to use their intelligence to work and share the joy of improving their company's productivity.

NPS believes in the importance of every improvement, no matter how minor. Very often, suggestions for improvement are not made because management will not pay attention to them, or because the suggester is blamed for suggestions that fail while management takes credit for the ones that work. With NPS, however, each suggester gets credit for his or her suggestion, and a suggestion that is adopted on the shop floors is referred to as "Mr. or Ms. so-and-so's method." This practice motivates workers to use their heads. Moreover, because all workers are told that NPS belongs to everybody and that its purpose is to make everyone's job easier and better paid, improvement suggestions come from part-time as well as full-time workers. Exceptional suggestions are rewarded accordingly. When everyone understands that NPS allows the workers to improve the workplace, the workplace truly comes alive.

Persuasion through Clever Analogies

Getting workers and managers to understand that all employees can and must make an effort to improve the workplace is not easy. It is a path that crosses mountains and valleys. It was mentioned earlier that those on the production floors are usually more willing to accept NPS than those in management. It is quite common, however, for there initially to be very strong resistance on the shop floors. Because NPS believes that division of labor is an impediment to the smooth flow of work and that separatism breeds stagnation, many tasks previously performed sitting down are now required to be done standing. This is because a worker must usually be standing up to perform a multiplicity of tasks. For example, it is difficult to help the overburdened worker next to you when you are sitting down.

But convincing a group of workers to stand while doing a job previously done sitting down is difficult. The workers regard this as an increase in their work load. And when you top it off by saying that each worker must oversee three or four machines or processes, workers naturally resent this and say that one task at a time is enough, and that doing so many things at once will be confusing.

However, workers start to understand when NPS points out that although it may seem like conventional wisdom that working while seated is more comfortable, a different wisdom holds that working while standing up is much healthier and less tiring than sitting all day. Workers start to believe this. It is indeed true that sitting down all day can cause lower back pain and tense shoulders. A job that must be performed standing up is usually far less routine and much healthier.

To persuade the workers that work performed standing up is more productive than work performed sitting down, the NPS instructors cite the example of a housewife. The example is clear:

> Does a housewife sit down when she is cooking or washing clothes? Of course not. She stands up. What do you think would happen if she did them sitting down? She would not be able to do the jobs as smoothly. It is only because she is standing up that she can keep an eye on the meal cooking on the stove while preparing the salad and setting the table. The housewife doesn't say she wants to do them sitting down, does she? Well, let's work like the housewife and see how productivity increases.

NPS instructors are good storytellers. By standing up, a one-talent worker becomes multi-talented like the housekeeper who cooks, does laundry, cleans the house, mends clothes, and looks after children. The NPS instructors say it is debasing to people's dignity to let them perform only one thing or to say that they are able to do only one thing. People are, by nature, multi-talented. Superiors who do not utilize their workers' full potential are not doing their jobs.

There is nothing more wonderful for a worker than to be allowed to develop his or her talents. We all have tremendous potential and yearn to have it recognized. However, in many companies, the workers are nothing but cogs in a big wheel who must work day in and day out, in the background, and out of the limelight. When people work only for money, they do not find meaning in their work.

How would it be if your own ideas and those of your colleagues were adopted in your workplace and you could see tangible improvements in the workplace every day, or every three days or week or month or six months or year? When the workers see that changes occur in their workplace not because the changes are ordered from above but because they and their fellow workers are voluntarily devising them, they become committed to their jobs. Workers are usually not receptive to ideas forced upon them. Presented with ideas from their peers, they are usually willing to try them even though they may be far from perfect. This receptiveness helps the potential of each worker to be eventually realized.

When people are moved to action only on orders from above or for monetary gain, they usually harbor a false obedience. However, when people perceive that their talents are appreciated and that the system will reward their accomplishments fairly, they exhibit unexpected abilities. NPS does not try to coerce people into increasing their productivity. The NPS movement increases the productivity of the workplace by recognizing the ability of the workers.

The Twenty-Five Doctrines of NPS

An interesting thing happens once you start utilizing the abilities of each worker. Myths such as "only so-and-so can do that job" or "it's best to let only him do that job" are shattered. This shows that many tasks thought to be difficult are actually easy and that many people can do a better job than the so-called experts.

There are people in managerial positions who like to boss people around. Many of these arrogant types do not realize that it is their position and not themselves as individuals that allows them to boss people around. They may have reached the position not through ability but simply by being there long enough or by knowing the right people. Individuals like this can have a nervous breakdown, develop an ulcer, or have their hair turn white when they lose their title or when NPS appears on the scene. The reason may be that their status is diminished.

According to Suzumura, this sort of reaction is understandable because it is like someone who has spent an entire life in the mountains suddenly having to live on the beach.

NPS has a set of rules called the "Twenty-five Doctrines of NPS." Some of these rules are cited below because they give a good idea of how the member companies start out.

- Don't make excuses.
- Think of how to do it, not how to explain it.
- Don't worry too much about what might happen.
- Do it now.
- Problems beget wisdom.
- Don't seek perfection. 60 percent is good enough. Move forward.
- Try the NPS method for at least a year before complaining.
- Replace activities that don't contribute to profits with ones that do.
- Time is the shadow of motion.
- Don't use money. Use your head. If you can't use your head, use your body.
- There is always room for improvement.
- Debunk the myths.

Eliminating the Searchers

With NPS, the transformation of employees into multi-talented workers begins with assigning two or more machines to each worker. The basic philosophy is that a worker can operate one machine while another is running by itself.

Take for example Nippon Light Metal's Osaka plant, which before NPS stepped in was suffering from the triple burden of high cost, poor sales, and a high defect rate. Before NPS arrived, 140 workers were producing 15,000 capacitors a month at the plant. The NPS instructors felt that even 70 employees were too many.

Reducing the number of workers was obviously the first thing to do in order to make the operation profitable. However, reducing the number of workers could not mean overtime or a greater work load on the remaining workers. This is in line with one of NPS's basic tenets: do not waste the precious time of workers, who have only one life to live.

Then how can the number of workers be reduced? One important solution is *multiple-process responsibility*. In almost any factory, each process functions independently of the other processes. Work-in-process starts piling up all over the factory, the walls become filled with parts, and the entire factory becomes a mess. These factories use appointed "searchers" who look for parts, saying: "That part is supposed to be there" or "This part is supposed to be here." The searcher has to look for parts, stack and unstack them from shelves, and otherwise engage in tasks that add no value to the end product (this means that customers cannot be directly charged for the tasks).

NPS does not regard looking for things and stacking and unstacking parts as real work. It does not tolerate tasks that do not add value. The first thing NPS did at the Osaka plant was to eliminate the appointed searchers and movers. It is understood that if each process only produced what was needed by a later process and only when required in the amount needed, the goods would flow smoothly without having to be looked for or unnecessarily stacked and unstacked.

Next, the production lines were modified at the Osaka plant. Unnecessary belt conveyors were eliminated, and the plant layout was changed to facilitate worker movement. Equipment was modified — without spending too much money —

for easier use. What was pursued was not automation but greater equipment autonomy to enable one worker to oversee more equipment and more processes.

In six months after the start of the improvement project, the number of workers on the capacitor production line at Nippon Light Metal's Osaka plant was reduced from 140 to 80, and this work-force reduction continues. During the same period, productivity more than tripled, and the lot size was reduced from the previous 500 capacitors to 100.

Because the earlier processes must produce only when the parts are actually demanded by the subsequent processes, it is necessary for labor, equipment, and material to be ready for action when an order is received from a subsequent process. If the orders issued by the subsequent processes fluctuate widely in terms of delivery deadline or order quantity, the earlier processes must always have at their disposal the labor, equipment and material for sustaining a peak load. However, staying ready for a peak load is the single greatest source of waste. The practice is bound to increase production costs.

Therefore, the subsequent processes must provide the earlier processes with information concerning demand as soon as possible and must make the order volume uniform so that the work load on the earlier processes is leveled out. Salespeople tend to sign orders at the end of the month and demand that deadlines be met. It is understandable that the production floors cannot meet the requirements and that this practice only leads to increased friction between the sales departments and the production floors. To ensure the success of the NPS production method based on kanban and the philosophy of later processes determining the output of the earlier processes, it is vitally important for the later processes to do their utmost to level out the production demand.

Reducing Set-Up Time

An important factor in producing in lot sizes of one, that is, in alternately producing different items instead of the same thing over and over, is the speed with which the equipment setup can be changed. One reason mass production reduces cost is that it allows many items to be produced, once a time-consuming setup is accomplished.

For example, assume that it takes one hour to change an equipment setup, during which time the equipment remains idle and is wasted. If the equipment setup is changed four times a day, the equipment is idle four hours every day. Conventional wisdom says that it is better to reduce the number of set-up changes, in this case, from four to three, three to two, and two to one.

If you try to recoup your original expense using one set-up change, you tend to overproduce to reduce cost. Assume that an equipment's setup is changed once a day in order to maximize the running time of the equipment, but also that different products must be produced, which would require three set-up changes. Since only one change is done, this would require the purchase of new equipment — a form of waste — to handle the different product requirements.

The situation changes if the set-up time can be significantly reduced. If the set-up time is reduced to 15 minutes, changing the setup four times takes only one hour. This would allow the equipment to handle four different product types. If the set-up time can be reduced to one minute, 60 set-up changes can be accomplished in one hour, and the same number of products can be produced in one day as when it took an hour to change the setup once a day. In other words, one important condition for producing in lot sizes of one and achieving high-diversity, small-lot production is to reduce the set-up time. NPS instructors set high goals. They challenge workers to reduce the set-up time from one hour to one minute.

When the NPS instructors first went to the Tokyo Plant of Nozawa, where it produced Asrock (a type of plain concrete pillars), the dies were being changed once or twice a week, which took an hour every time. The aim was to reduce cost by reducing the number of set-up changes and by producing as much as possible using a single set of dies.

However, this practice made production inflexible, and Nozawa lost many small orders. Its policy was not to accept any order smaller than 24 pillars since it did not pay. This policy was continued even after Nozawa had suffered a loss of nearly ¥600 million ($2.4 million) three years earlier.

The NPS instructors demanded that the set-up time be reduced to one minute. Those on the production floors resisted adamantly, calling the demand impossible. However, the instructors methodically eliminated waste from all operations involved in changing the setup. The location of the tools used for changing the setup, the distances involved, the method for undoing the previous setup, the way nuts were tightened, and every motion of the workers, were analyzed. Precious seconds were removed from each operation.

As a result of these improvements, the time required for changing the setup was reduced by 90 percent, from 60 minutes to 6 minutes; 54 minutes of previously wasted time were eliminated from the plant operations. The number of set-up changes per month at Nozawa's Asrock line went from 39 in 1983, immediately before joining NPS, to 208 in July 1985. The number of minor set-up changes performed for accommodating different sizes of the same model increased from 397 to 2,205.

The delivery time, previously 30 days, was reduced to five days including transportation to the customer's site. The minimum lot size was reduced from 24 pillars to 3 and the inventory was reduced from 45,000 pillars to 10,000.

At the Yamagata plant of Ihara Koatsu Tsugite, the time required for changing the setup of a large Japanese machine was reduced from two hours to 27 minutes by mid-1985. To accomplish this, workers underwent training until one or two in the morning, until their bodies and minds had memorized the operation. NPS was not satisfied: they know that there is always room for improvement.

A thread-winding machine, manufactured by Gildmeister of West Germany — acknowledged as the best of its kind — is installed at Ihara's Daijin Plant. The equipment manufacturer specifies a set-up changing time of anywhere from 8 to 24 hours, under certain circumstances. At Ihara Koatsu, however, the set-up changing time is not just less than one hour or even 30 minutes, but less than 15 minutes. The present goal is three minutes. The cost incurred in reducing the set-up changing time to 30 minutes was zero. The expense allowed for modifications is limited to ¥10,000 ($40), no matter what.

Product Diversity: The NPS Market Advantage

Should we believe that the age of volume sales of single products is over? Or that reducing production cost by mass production and selling in large quantities at a slim profit margin will remain the basic principle of business? There will probably always be proponents of each view. But which is correct? The question is already being answered and time will only make the answer more obvious.

In the auto industry, GM, Ford, and Chrysler — the followers of mass production — have suffered hard blows from Toyota. And Nissan is no longer Toyota's rival. We must not forget that Toyota's success and its greatest strength is based on Toyota's decision not to compete with GM and Ford in terms of mass production, but to base its business on catering to the diverse needs and desires of its customers.

There is no doubt that Japan is turning into a very advanced information society. Although some feel that the information age will mean uniformity and standardization of society, the contrary seems true. The information age is breeding greater diversity and individualism, which consumers express in the products they buy. As the speed of information propagation increases, people feel a need to express their individuality to avoid feeling left behind. Affluence permits this diversity and individualism, while poverty denies the luxury of individual expression.

In the world of fashion, it is said that the rest of Japan is more sensitive that Tokyo to the latest fashion. One reason may be that people living outside of Tokyo have the illusion that what they see on TV is actually popular in Tokyo. On the other hand, what is fashionable in the countryside is ignored in Tokyo. With such diversity, standardization and uniformity are increasingly difficult to sell. NPS's philosophy and its production method are powerful weapons that will help companies survive in the coming age of consumer demand for diversity.

Is it easy to transplant NPS's philosophy or production method into a company? The answer is no. Of course, trying is welcome, and the determination and courage to try are highly respected. However, total commitment is required for success. One should remember the proverb: "A little learning is a dangerous thing."

Vigilance Is the Price of Continuing Success

The number of NPS members will probably continue to increase. However, those seeking membership should not think that success is guaranteed just because other companies have experienced success after joining. For NPS methods to succeed, top management must have strong commitment. Moreover, the member company must have a strong program for incorporating the NPS method and philosophy into its own structure, and for making sure that it firmly takes root in the company.

Using the NPS method and philosophy does provide quick results such as greater space availability, reduced inventory, reduced indebtedness, and a rapid increase in productivity. However, it is after these initial benefits are obtained that the greatest danger arises. If you become complacent and let down your guard, the factions within the company favoring the old system may strike back and force a return to the old ways. Once this happens, it is very difficult to restructure the company anew.

NPS is an endless effort. Complacency can be fatal. Remember the proverb: "A small leak can sink a great ship." What NPS fears most is that companies will fulfill the proverb: "The danger past, God is forgotten." The company that transforms itself with NPS methods must keep using them to improve itself if it is to continue to reap the benefits. Companies that do keep the NPS methods working vitally throughout their organizations will find themselves among the most competitive companies in an age of increasingly diverse demands from consumers.

About the Author

*I*N 1985, Isao Shinohara was
named Deputy Editor-in-Chief
of *Shukan Toyo Kenzai (Weekly Toyo Kenzai)*, Japan's foremost financial newspaper. Since 1986 he has served as Editor-in-Chief of the publication *All Tohshi (All Investment)*. He is also the author of a major book, *Kabushiki Kakumei (Stock Revolution)*. This is his first book to be published in English.

Index

BOOKS BY TAIICHI OHNO

TOYOTA PRODUCTION SYSTEM: Beyond Large-Scale Production
by Taiichi Ohno
The "father" of Just-In-Time describes the origins and philosophy behind the most revolutionary manufacturing system since Henry Ford. The first book written on the Toyota Production System, Ohno's classic is now available in English for the first time.
ISBN 0-915299-14-3 / March 1988 / $39.95

WORKPLACE MANAGEMENT
by Taiichi Ohno
An in-depth view of how one of this century's leading industrial thinkers approaches problem solving and continuous improvement. Gleaned from Ohno's forty years of experimentation and innovation in the workplace, this book explains the concepts that Ohno considers to be most important to successful management.
ISBN 0-915299-19-4 / March 1988 / $34.95

JUST-IN-TIME FOR TODAY AND TOMORROW
by Taiichi Ohno and Stetsuo Mito
Taiichi Ohno's latest ideas are brought out in this discussion of JIT management and its application to every kind of workplace. A lively dialogue between Ohno and journalist Mito, covering topics like how easily JIT and kanban fit into this "information age," leadership imagination and decisiveness, and 7-Eleven food stores.
ISBN 0-915299-20-8 / August 1988 / $34.95

Productivity Press, Dept. BK, P.O. Box 3007, Cambridge, MA 02140   617/497-5146

OTHER BOOKS ON JUST-IN-TIME

NEW PRODUCTION SYSTEM: JIT Crossing Industry Boundaries
by Isao Shinohara
The most popular book on JIT in Japan today. Incorporating the ideas of Taiichi Ohno, it shows how NPS works in a broad range of industries, including a garment factory, a fast food chain, and a lumber company. Differences in product are no excuse for the waste found in most manufacturing plants; see how to reevaluate business methods from the very root in order to achieve extremely efficient production.
ISBN 0-915299-21-6 / May 1988 / $34.95

NON-STOCK PRODUCTION: The Shingo System for
Continuous Improvement
by Shigeo Shingo
Shingo, who developed JIT at Toyota with Taiichi Ohno, teaches how to implement non-stock production in your JIT manufacturing operations. The culmination of his extensive writings on efficient production management and continuous improvement, his latest book is an essential companion volume to previous books on other key elements of JIT, including SMED and Poka-Yoke.
ISBN 0-915299-30-5 / June 1988 / $75.00

KANBAN AND JUST-IN-TIME AT TOYOTA:
Management Begins at the Workplace
edited by the Japan Management Association, translated by David J. Lu
Based on seminars given by Taiichi Ohno, "father" of the Just-In-Time system, this book goes far beyond JIT to explore the philosophy and makeup of the most efficient and productive organization in the world. It is perfect for the first stage of JIT implementation.
ISBN 0-915299-08-9 / 168 pages / $29.95

THE CANON PRODUCTION SYSTEM:
Creative Involvement of the Total Workforce
compiled by the Japan Management Association
A fantastic success story! Canon set a goal to increase productivity by three percent per month — and achieved it! The first book-length case study to show how a large company can combine the most effective Japanese management principles and techniques into one overall strategy that improves every area of the company.
ISBN 0-915299-06-2 / 232 pages / $36.95

Productivity Press, Dept. BK, P.O. Box 3007, Cambridge, MA 02140 617/497-5146

BOOKS AVAILABLE FROM PRODUCTIVITY PRESS

Christopher, William F. **Productivity Measurement Handbook**
ISBN 0-915299-05-4 / 1983 / 680 pages / looseleaf / $137.95

Fukuda, Ryuji. **Managerial Engineering: Techniques for Improving Quality and Productivity in the Workplace**
ISBN 0-915299-09-7 / 1984 / 206 pages / hardcover / $34.95

Hatakeyama, Yoshio. **Manager Revolution! A Guide to Survival in Today's Changing Workplace**
ISBN 0-915299-10-0 / 1984 / 198 pages / hardcover / $24.95

Japan Management Association and Constance E. Dyer. **Canon Production System: Creative Involvement of the Total Workforce**
ISBN 0-915299-06-2 / 1987 / 251 pages / hardcover / $36.95

Japan Management Association. **Kanban and Just-In-Time at Toyota: Management Begins at the Workplace,** *translated by David J. Lu*
ISBN 0-915299-08-9 / 1986 / 186 pages / hardcover / $29.95

Lu, David J. **Inside Corporate Japan: The Art of Fumble-Free Management**
ISBN 0-915299-16-X / 1987 / 278 pages / hardcover / $24.95

Ohno, Taiichi. **Toyota Production System: Beyond Large-Scale Production**
ISBN 0-915299-14-3 / 1988 / 176 pages / hardcover / $39.95

Ohno, Taiichi. **Workplace Management**
ISBN 0-915299-19-4 / 1988 / 176 pages / hardcover / $34.95

Shingo, Shigeo. **A Revolution in Manufacturing: The SMED System,** *translated by Andrew P. Dillon*
ISBN 0-915299-03-8 / 1985 / 383 pages / hardcover / $65.00

Shingo, Shigeo. **Zero Quality Control: Source Inspection and the Poka-Yoke System,** *translated by Andrew P. Dillon*
ISBN 0-915299-07-0 / 1986 / 328 pages / hardcover / $65.00

Shingo, Shigeo. **The Sayings of Shigeo Shingo: Key Strategies for Plant Improvement,** *translated by Andrew P. Dillon*
ISBN 0-915299-15-1 / 1987 / 207 pages / hardcover / $36.95

AUDIO-VISUAL PROGRAMS

Shingo, Shigeo. **The SMED System,** *translated by Andrew P. Dillon*
ISBN 0-915299-11-9 / slides / $749.00
ISBN 0-915299-27-5 / video / $749.00

Shingo, Shigeo. **The Poka-Yoke System,** *translated by Andrew P. Dillon*
ISBN 0-915299-13-5 / slides / $749.00
ISBN 0-915299-28-3 / video / $749.00

Productivity Press, Dept. BK, P.O. Box 3007, Cambridge, MA 02140   617/497-5146

SPRING / SUMMER BOOKS FROM PRODUCTIVITY PRESS

Ford, Henry. **Today and Tomorrow** (originally published 1926)
ISBN 0-915299-36-4 / May 1988 / $24.95

Karatsu, Hajime. **TQC Wisdom of Japan: Managing for Total Quality Control**
ISBN 0-915299-18-6 / June 1988 / $34.95

Karatsu, Hajime. **Tough Words for American Industry**
ISBN 0-915299-25-9 / May 1988 / $24.95

Mizuno, Shigeru (ed.) **Management for Quality Improvement: The 7 New QC Tools**
ISBN 0-915299-29-1 / May 1988 / $59.95 (tent.)

Ohno, Taiichi and Setsuo Mito. **Just-In-Time for Today and Tomorrow: A Total Management System**
ISBN 0-915299-20-8 / August 1988 / $34.95 (tent.)

Shingo, Shigeo. **Non-Stock Production: The Shingo System for Continuous Improvement**
ISBN 0-915299-30-5 / June 1988 / $75.00

Shinohara, Isao. **New Production System: JIT Crossing Industry Boundaries**
ISBN 0-915299-21-6 / May 1988 / $34.95

TO ORDER: Write, phone or fax Productivity Press, Dept. BK, P.O. Box 3007, Cambridge, MA 02140, phone 617/497-5146, fax 617/868-3524. Send check or charge to your credit card (American Express, Visa, MasterCard accepted). Include street address for UPS delivery.

U.S. ORDERS: Add $3 shipping for first book, $1 each additional. CT residents add 7.5% and MA residents 5% sales tax. Add $5 for each AV.

FOREIGN ORDERS: Payment must be made in U.S. dollars. For Canadian orders, add $8 shipping for first book, $2 each additional. Orders to other countries are on a proforma basis; please indicate shipping method desired.

NOTE: Prices subject to change without notice.

Productivity Press, Dept. BK, P.O. Box 3007, Cambridge, MA 02140   617/497-5146